CELEBRATING A
CENTURY
SAINT MICHAEL'S COLLEGE

WDG PUBLISHING

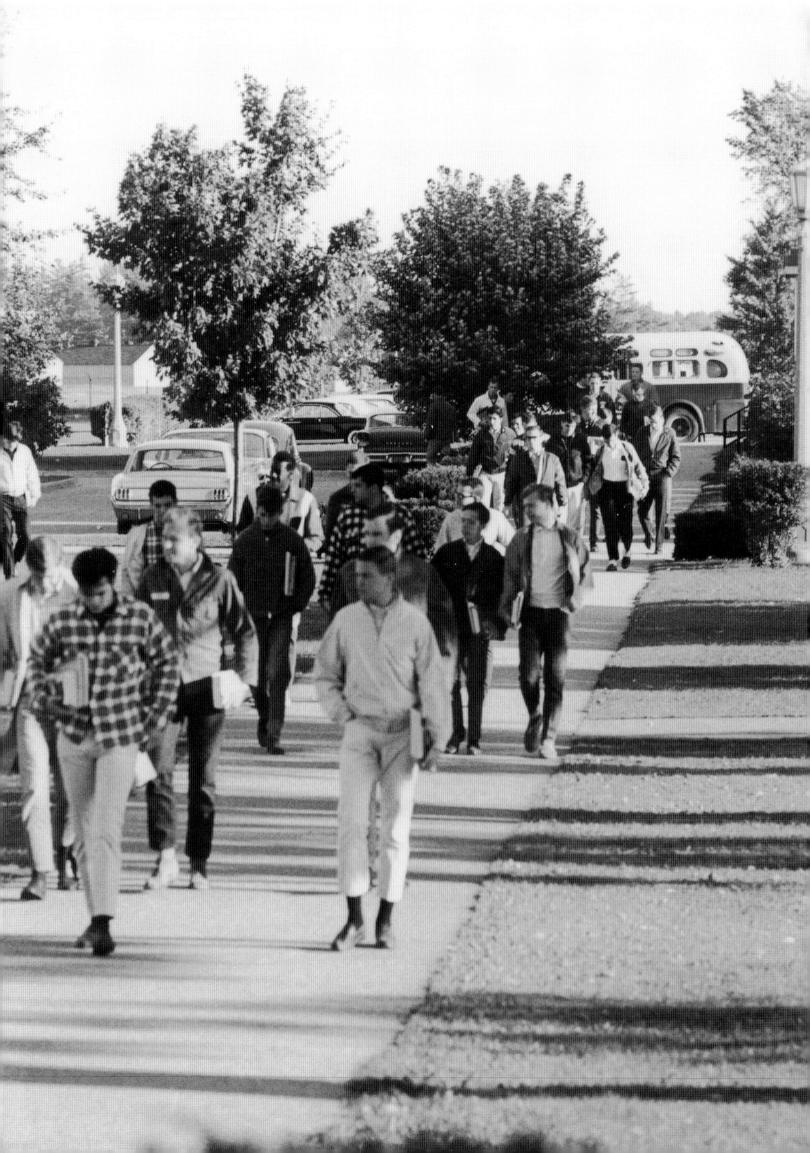

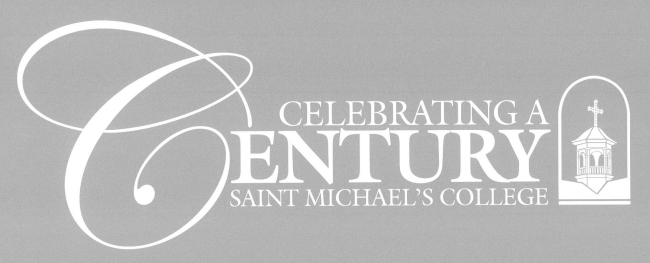

CELEBRATING A CENTURY
SAINT MICHAEL'S COLLEGE

1904 - 2004

PUBLISHED BY WDG PUBLISHING

Frontispiece: A group of Michaelmen make their way across campus, circa 1968.

CELEBRATING A
CENTURY
SAINT MICHAEL'S COLLEGE
1904-2004

Creative Direction   Duane Wood
Design/Art Direction   Sam Otis

First published in the United States of America by

WDG Communications Inc.
3500 F Avenue NW
Post Office Box 9573
Cedar Rapids, Iowa 52409-9573
Telephone (319) 396-1401
Facsimile (319) 396-1647

Library of Congress Cataloging-in-Publication Data

Celebrating a century, Saint Michael's College, 1904-2004 / [creative
direction, Duane Wood ; design/art direction, Sam Otis].
        p. cm.
Includes index.
   ISBN 0-9718323-2-3 (alk. paper)
   1. Saint Michael's College (Colchester, Vt.)--History. 2. Saint
Michael's College (Colchester, Vt.)--Pictorial works. I. Wood, Duane.
II. Otis, Sam.
   LD4821.S922C45 2003
   378.743'17--dc22

                                        2003023046

Printed in the United States of America

10 9 8 7 6 5 4 3 2 1

TABLE OF CONTENTS

BEGINNINGS

Marc A. vanderHeyden, *President*

The story of Saint Michael's College begins long before 1904, when the institution opened its doors for the first time to educate young men of Vermont. In the nineteenth century, a small group of French priests came together to form a religious community, and the story of our College flows from their lives devoted to service, God and the Church. However, these religious men in Burgundy, France, drew their inspiration from an even earlier time, from an English saint of the thirteenth century, who would eventually become the namesake for the Society of Saint Edmund, the founding order of Saint Michael's College.

When Saint Edmund crossed the English Channel as a young man to go to Paris and study the liberal arts, he unwittingly became a model for many thousands of American college students who now travel to Europe and elsewhere in the world for a junior year abroad. Despite the passage of almost 900 years, it is meaningful to juxtapose the image of Saint Edmund sailing across the Channel in the late twelfth century with students at Saint Michael's College in the twenty-first century traveling across the oceans for the purpose of learning. While Saint Edmund was clear in his direct pursuit of the liberal arts, our students are more inclined to undertake a semester or more abroad as

◆ (facing page) Statue of Saint Edmund ◆ (left) Plaque about Saint Edmund

Dana Lim vanderHeyden

Pitkin Unichrome Ltd.

Dana Lim vanderHeyden

◆ (above) The spires of Oxford University. Around 1181, Edmund Rich and his brother left home to attend the grammar school at Oxford. While at Oxford, Edmund "met the Christ-like child while walking alone through the fields," an encounter that began Edmund's life-long practice of tracing the name 'Jesus' on his forehead before bed each night as the Christ-child had instructed. In 1190, Edmund left Oxford for Paris where he received his master's degree after studying the master of arts curriculum. Edmund returned to Oxford as a teacher of geometry and, in 1195, introduced the English university to "new Aristotelian learning." Six years later he returned to Paris to study theology and to be ordained. From 1213-14 until 1222, Edmund taught at Oxford University before becoming overseer of the Cathedral at Salisbury. ◆ (left) Main Entrance to Saint Edmund's Hall at Oxford: Saint Edmund's Hall is the last remaining medieval hall at Oxford University. Founded as a residence hall in the early thirteenth century, it is located in the parish of St.-Peter-in-the-East, where Edmund Rich, Archbishop of Canterbury, lived and taught. Saint Edmund's coat of arms, which is above the entrance, portrays the Saint Edmund cross as well as four Cornish choughs, a variety of crow with red legs and beak. The inscription on the lintel, SANCTVS EDMVNDVS HVIVS AVLAE LVX ("Saint Edmund, the Light of this Hall"), also reveals, by means of the chronogram, the date of his canonization, 1246. ◆ (right) Window at College Saint Michel in Château-Gontier featuring Reverend Amand Prével, who became the first president of Saint Michael's College.

a result of their study of the liberal arts, in order to enhance their learning and living experience on campus with a variety of adventures, encounters and enrichments in far-flung corners of the world.

The desire for knowledge continues to be as strong as it was nine centuries ago and is certainly more varied now. Thus, we do well as an institution of higher learning to keep Saint Edmund as a model for the broad-based educational experience that Saint Michael's College provides.

When Edmund of Abingdon returned home from Paris, he studied at Oxford and became one of the founders of a residential college there, subsequently called Saint Edmund's Hall. He was the first doctor of theology at the same university, where he served as a teacher and scholar for many years.

He pursued an ecclesiastical career, serving as a parish curate in the small town of Calne and subsequently as treasurer of the Cathedral of Salisbury, where he learned a great deal about finances and other practical matters that were not part of a spiritual life. Eventually, he was chosen to be Archbishop of Canterbury, and while he welcomed the prospect of living in a community, he soon realized that this experience, too, was filled with difficulties and tribulations. In Edmund's case, he tried earnestly to combine the leadership role assigned to him with the humble life of a monk, and it proved to be a challenge.

Because of some very serious disputes between himself and the canons of the cathedral, as well as some imminent conflicts with the king, Edmund as Archbishop crossed the Channel once again, this time to visit Rome. On the way, he stopped at the Cistercian abbey of Pontigny, where he felt not only welcome, but very much at home because of the contemplative and quiet nature of the community, so different from the hustle and bustle of the university town of Oxford and the troubled situation in the Cathedral of Canterbury.

According to modern historiography, it is not certain whether Edmund died on his trip to the Vatican or on the way back to England, but we do know he requested that his body be returned to Pontigny. There, in the abbey church, he was laid to rest. Very shortly thereafter, Edmund was declared a saint of the Church.

The Cistercians of Pontigny were blessed to live, learn and pray in a wonderful monastic environment, endowed with one of the most beautiful abbatial churches in France. Nevertheless, the community went through tremendous ups and downs throughout the centuries. The religious wars brought confusion and destruction, and also paralyzed the spirit that had first engendered the creation of this magnificent medieval monastery.

◆ (below) The exterior of Pontigny Abbey. In October 1240, Edmund was traveling to Rome and became ill, stopping his travel at the Cistercian monastery in Pontigny, France, where he asked to be buried. He died in the town of Sens, only about 50 miles from Pontigny, on November 16, 1240. His body was returned to Pontigny, where he was buried. In 1843, a group of priests who would later become the Society of Saint Edmund established a community at Pontigny. ◆ (facing page) Pontigny Abbey Interior

After the Reformation, the Cistercians at Pontigny gave way to a much more lax adherence to the rule of Saint Benedict, and it was not surprising that the abbey was decimated during the French Revolution. Not only was the property confiscated and distributed among a variety of parties, but many buildings were dismantled and the materials used in other constructions throughout the region. The monastery lay in ruins until the middle of the century.

In the 1840s, Father Muard, who would become the founder of the Society of Saint Edmund, inquired of the Bishop of Sens as to whether he could locate a new group of young priests in a religious community and occupy some parts of the abbey. When permission was given, this early group of religious began restoration of the church and renewed its devotion to Saint Edmund, who was buried there. Known as auxiliary priests, they worked in several parts of France. In the latter part of the century, they were invited to go to Mont-Saint-Michel, where they helped with both the ministry and in rebuilding that most famous of Benedictine abbeys in France.

Terryl Kinder

Terryl Kinder

The priests of Saint Edmund were beloved in their respective ministries, but anticlerical laws at the turn of the century forced them out of the country. A decade before, a fair number had already migrated to Vermont, where they had established a settlement with a house of study in Swanton.

The Edmundites were invited by the Bishop of Burlington to start a school in the area. They agreed, and in 1902, purchased the Michael Kelly farm in Winooski Park. The Society then added new construction to the farmhouse that permitted them to open Saint Michael's Institute in September 1904. The founders of Saint Michael's—Father Prével, Father Salmon, Father Total and Father Jeanmarie—were assisted by one lay teacher in educating a small group of students, who moved into the building we now call Founders Hall.

◆ The celebrated Benedictine abbey of Mont-Saint-Michel, founded in the eighth century, rises from a cone-shaped rock in the Bay of Saint-Malo, off the coast of Normandy, France. The Edmundites served as caretakers of the abbey from 1867 to 1886 and remained on the island until they were expelled from France as a result of the enactment of the anticlerical laws of 1901. Many found their way to Vermont.

These French priests were driven by faith, courage and an absolute commitment to the education of young people. They had no background in American higher education and still had difficulty with the language, but they devoted lives of hard work and prayer to the creation of what would become Saint Michael's College.

The early years were not easy, but the Society persevered and, with the help of friends in the local community—and, even more importantly, the direct and full assistance of their students—they developed an authentic American school environment. Indeed, some of the early hardships, and the tentative hold of higher education in the New World, led to long-standing traditions at Saint Michael's College.

For example, lacking any kind of experience with American education, the French priests had to rely on their students to create the community's extracurricular life. From the very beginning, students were given significant responsibility for all activities outside the classroom or laboratory. This practice is still very much alive at our College and has proved to be vital in creating the collegiate spirit that characterizes Saint Michael's.

◆ (above) First Edmundites in Vermont: In 1891, two members of the Society of Saint Edmund, Reverend Alexis Videloup and Brother J. Galette, traveled to North America in an attempt to find sites for new apostolates free from the strife of France. The Sulpicians of Montreal directed them to the Bishop of Burlington, Vermont, Bishop DeGoesbriand, and he offered them an assignment on the islands of Lake Champlain. Videloup was installed at Keeler's Bay, where he served for three years. Reverend Amand Prével, SSE, visited the United States on September 16, 1895 to consult the bishop on a foundation of the Community in the United States. The Bishop agreed to give the Nativity of Our Lady parish in Swanton, Vermont, to the Edmundites. Within three years, a juniorate, or apostolic school, was established in Swanton with four students. Pictured are members of Society of Saint Edmund, many of whom arrived in September of 1902, following the purchase of the Michael Kelly farm in Winooski Park: Brother Landrin, Brother Cheray, Brother Jeanmarie, Reverend Fricot, Brother Herrouet, Brother Total, Brother Lequellec, Brother Nicolle, Brother Ledoux, and Brother Renard. ◆ (below) The Kelly farmhouse before construction of Founders Hall.

The Edmundites were highly disciplined, deeply devoted and embraced a liberal arts tradition. Hence, the early programs–in addition to being bilingual, which made them rather unique for the College's first two decades–provided coursework in the classics, along with offerings that were preparatory for an immediate career. These commercial programs are analogous to what we would probably refer to as the business department today.

In many ways, the early Edmundite community at Saint Michael's preserved the long tradition of the intellectual life of the Church that they had known in France. At the same time, they looked to the future and presented their students with the opportunity to engage in learning that would afford them the opportunity for employment upon graduation. In so doing, they established an academic ethos at Saint Michael's College that has endured for a century: faithfulness to an intellectual tradition and practical preparation for the future. ◆

◆ On March 3, 1903, the Articles of Association of Saint Michael's Institute were filed with Vermont's Secretary of State. The articles encompassed all the foundations and property of the Society of Saint Edmund in the United States. ◆ (facing page) Reverend Amand Prével: In August 1903, Superior General Laproste asked Reverend Aubin, Superior of the Saint Michael's and Swanton houses, to take over a new school venture in Hitchin, England. On October 7, 1903, Rev. Prével arrived to take over Saint Michael's.

◆ (above) Reverend Aubin had purchased the Kelly farm property for $5,500 with $1,000 payable immediately. The property, including the farm house pictured above, was deeded to Saint Michael's Institute on July 30, 1903. ◆ (below) Construction initiatives had been undertaken by Rev. Aubin prior to his departure, but a loan request for $25,000 was rejected by Bishop Michaud. Rev. Prével, too, tried to secure a loan and Rev. Laproste soon authorized Prével to borrow $15,000. Construction began in May of 1904 and continued throughout the summer on a $19,046.18 building that could accommodate as many as 50 boarders. The new building was dedicated on September 29, 1904, blessed by Bishop Michaud.

◆ (above) The student body and faculty in 1905: Front row: Professor G. Ferris, Brother Honorat, F.I.C., Reverend Eugene Labory, Very Reverend Amand Prével, Reverend Louis M. Cheray, Reverend Alan Lequellec, Brother Felix, F.I.C., and Professor C.E. Bellemare. Second row, at far right: Reverend C. Hanfield. Third row, at left: Reverend J.M. Herrouet. Third row, at far right: Reverend William Jeanmarie. Center of fourth row: Reverend Ernest Salmon. ◆ (left) Early Diploma: Saint Michael's held its first graduation on June 21, 1907. The four students who successfully completed the college course received diplomas. The College could not grant degrees until Vermont Governor Allen M. Fletcher signed the Act of Incorporation on January 28, 1913.

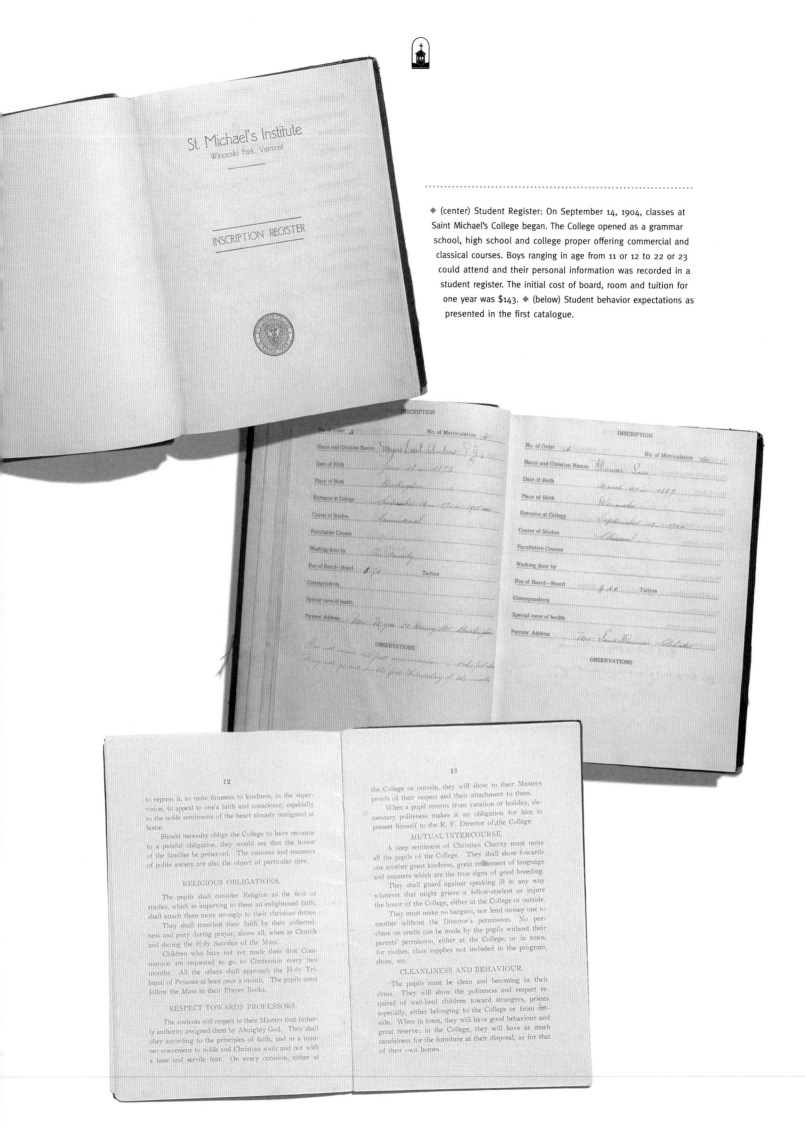

◆ (center) Student Register: On September 14, 1904, classes at Saint Michael's College began. The College opened as a grammar school, high school and college proper offering commercial and classical courses. Boys ranging in age from 11 or 12 to 22 or 23 could attend and their personal information was recorded in a student register. The initial cost of board, room and tuition for one year was $143. ◆ (below) Student behavior expectations as presented in the first catalogue.

◆ (above) Founders Hall, when completed in 1908, housed virtually all College functions, including the first dining hall, shown here in 1931. ◆ (below) Physical Training Class: Saint Michael's founders did not overlook the importance of physical training, although attention was paid to make sure students did not become overly engrossed in physical activity. By 1920, a physical training class was held four times per week at the close of the afternoon sessions. Work included calisthenics, marching and elements of military drills, with the aim of harmonious development of the body and the mind.

◆ Saint Michael's founders knew that activities would be important and within the first year had established a student Athletic Association board. Students used a dirt floor gymnasium in a small Founders Hall room and in 1905 organized and fielded the College's first baseball team. Front row: A. Pinard, L. Galipeau, W. Gelineau and T. Ryan. Middle row: G. Limoges and G. O'Brien. Back row: B. McMahon, E. Labory, T. Barttro, G. Ledoux and J. Pellerin.

◆ (above) The college student body increased at a rapid rate and soon outgrew its small building. Construction began to enlarge and reface the building on July 22, 1907. ◆ (below) Taken in the 1920s, this photograph shows Old Hall, today known as Founders Hall, as it looked for many years after the renovations and brick overlay in 1907. The exterior porch remained on the building until 1954.

◆ (above) 1917 Hockey Team ◆ (right) Saint Michael's first ski team, as identified on the photo as Dessert, F. John Stewart '52, Gosselin '52, and John O'Connell '51. ◆ (facing page) 1929-30 Basketball State Championship banner

TRANSFORMATION

Reverend Raymond J. Doherty, SSE '51

In 1947, my senior year of high school at Sacred Heart in Newton, Massachusetts, I applied late for Saint Michael's College. Because my basketball and baseball coach wrote a letter of recommendation on my behalf to his friend, coach Ron Corbett at Saint Michael's, I was placed on the "preferred waiting list." Fortunately, at literally the very last minute, I was informed on a Saturday morning that if I wanted to be a Saint Michael's student I should report to campus the following Monday. My parents gave their generous permission (they had to pay the bill), so I boarded a Vermont Transit bus out of Boston Sunday night and arrived at the door of Saint Michael's early Monday morning thinking that perhaps the bus driver might have made a mistake, since the barracks-adorned campus resembled more a military base than a college. I was barely seventeen years old at the time.

◆ (facing page) Early aerial shot of campus ◆ (below) In 1933, students gathered outside Saint Edmund's Hall, now known as Father Salmon Hall. Standing (left to right): Zenon Forcier, Jean-Paul Papineau, Casimir Cichanowicz, Albert Verrett, Lucien Lareau, John Stankiewicz, Leon Paulin, Paul Hébert, Leo Martel, David Bourgeois, and Henry Granger. Sitting: Lorenzo D'Agostino, Eugene Plante, Brother Aime Trahan, Reverend Eugene Alliot, Father Anthony McCue, unknown, and Norman Lambert. Many of those pictured graduated from Saint Edmund's Juniorate in Swanton and went on to become members of the Society of Saint Edmund.

L.L. McAlister

Thus began a wonderful four-year period that has profoundly affected the rest of my life, up to the present, some 55 years later. I came to Saint Michael's with few, if any, serious career plans. My main interest that freshman year was to play baseball for the College. I was uncertain of a major and at some point during the year a good friend in the class and I joined the newly formed Marine Corps Reserve unit in Burlington thinking, I suppose, that the United States Marines might be a career option.

One of the truly positive influences was the high percentage of World War II veterans on campus. These men, some of whom were married, were for the most part serious students taking advantage of the G.I. Bill, which enabled them to get an education that, without government funding, they probably could never have afforded. They were a mature breed, among whom were combat survivors, and their maturity was a great example for us youngsters.

Certainly, a watershed moment in my Saint Michael's College experience was a Shakespeare course I took in my sophomore year from the legendary

◆ (above) The five oldest Edmundites in America pause for a photograph outside of College Hall (Jeanmarie) in 1943: Reverend William Jeanmarie, Reverend Eugene Alliot, Reverend Victor Nicolle, Reverend John M. Herrouet, and Reverend Marie-Joseph Trigory. ◆ (below) Reverend Leon E. Gosselin, SSE, served as Saint Michael's sixth President from 1934 to 1940.

Jeremiah K. Durick '23, an all-time great among Saint Michael's professors. From that moment I began to appreciate the value of knowledge for its own sake and I became a serious student, not just mainly interested in baseball. I was eventually elected to Delta Epsilon Sigma, a national academic honor society, and to Who's Who Among American College and University Students, a tribute really to Professor Durick and other favorite teachers and friends who had inspired me, such as John Donoghue, Henry Fairbanks, Ed Murphy, Reverend Raymond Poirier, SSE, and Reverend Gerald Duford, SSE. Not to leave out, of course, our soft-spoken but dynamic College president, Reverend Daniel Lyons, SSE.

After that life-transforming sophomore year, I decided to major in English (a wise choice) with a

◆ (left) Saint Michael's seventh president, Reverend James H. Petty, SSE, kept the College on course with strong leadership during the difficult years of World War II. Enrollment had dropped from over 200 in 1940 to 37 by the third year of the war. ◆ (right) Reverend Daniel P. Lyons, SSE '26, served as Saint Michael's eighth president from 1946-1952 and oversaw the College's great post-war growth. The third quadrangle dormitory, Lyons Hall, was named in his honor in 1958.

personally chosen specialization in journalism (another very wise choice). In those days, Saint Michael's College did not offer a major in journalism, as it does now, but John Donoghue ("Mr. D."), an experienced journalist himself, taught an excellent two-semester course in journalism, which I devoured. At the same time, I was getting more involved with the college newspaper, *The Michaelman*, and became editor-in-chief in my senior year. As a senior, I was also awarded a scholarship by the College to serve as Mr. Donoghue's sports publicity assistant. And, yes, I did play baseball at Saint Michael's for another College legend, coach and athletic director George "Doc" Jacobs.

These happy undergraduate years came to an end with graduation in 1951 and, almost immediately in July 1951, service in the Marine Corps during the Korean War. My Saint Michael's College education prepared me well for that military service, as I was able to land a position in Marine Corps Public Information. Although I eventually earned the designation of "Combat Correspondent," I was, thank God, spared from being sent into combat in Korea.

In 1967, I returned to Saint Michael's College as a priest and as the director of Campus Ministry, succeeding the first officially designated campus minister at the College, Reverend Nelson Ziter, SSE (a little man, but he left behind huge shoes for me to try to fill). The thirteen years that I served in this position (1967-1980) were among the happiest and most satisfying of my professional life. Along the way, I also served as superior for six years of the Edmundite Community at Saint Michael's, and I happily continue to work part-time in the Edmundite Office of Campus Ministry. I also continue to be a member of the College's Board of Trustees (a total, thus far, of twenty-three non-consecutive years).

Naturally, over the fifty-plus years that I have been very personally associated with and involved in Saint Michael's, I have been witness to and part of many changes at the College. I cannot say for certain exactly which of the changes was the most important or the most significant, but surely one that has had a tremendous impact on Saint Michael's was the decision in the early 1970s, under President Bernard Boutin, to admit women. At the time, I was director of Campus Ministry at the College and very much in the midst of this major campus-altering change. It took foresight and courage to go this route, but the women at Saint Michael's College have, I am convinced, immensely helped the College to become a nationally recognized and highly respected liberal arts Catholic institution of higher learning. Amazingly, I think, the women undergraduates have, in a relatively short time,

Shortly after my return to civilian status (July 1953), I was accepted as a novice and student for the ordained priesthood in the Society of Saint Edmund. Needless to say, the Fathers and Brothers of the Society had made a profound impression on me during my undergraduate years at Saint Michael's. The Society's Vocation Director (later Superior General), Father Eymard Galligan, SSE, was a key figure in my decision to enter the novitiate.

◆ (above) Saint Michael's alumni killed in action during World War II.
◆ (facing page above) Following World War II, enrollment at colleges across the United States, including Saint Michael's, began to increase because of the passage of the G.I. Bill in 1944. The College acquired temporary housing from Fort Ethan Allen which was transported across the fields to its resting place at Saint Michael's. Here, workers

move a one-story building to its new home. Six of these buildings would become known as Miketown and were utilized mostly by married veterans. ◆ (facing page below) Besides bringing temporary barracks buildings to the campus to create "Miketown," other larger dormitory buildings were brought down from Fort Ethan Allen. Pictured here are Saint John's and Saint James halls, with Aquinas Hall on the left.

Detore Photo Service

come to outnumber their male counterparts. They are in the forefront of such valuable campus activities as volunteerism, campus ministry, student government and student publications. Although I am not a member of the faculty, I have no doubt that the young women shine in the classroom as well; and although, too, I enjoyed the all-male campus as an undergraduate myself, and later as a priest in campus ministry

serving these young men, I do not hesitate to acclaim that critical decision to become a coeducational college.

While still an undergraduate student at Saint Michael's, I saw the beginnings of the now ongoing physical changes at the College. By the end of my four years, the College had constructed Cheray Science Hall and the first of the quadrangle dormitories, Ryan Hall. The barracks and other former military buildings (dining room, auditorium and library) were gradually

Air Force ROTC
Det. 865
Saint Michael's College

becoming a thing of the past, yet a past they had served well, transitioning Saint Michael's from a truly small pre-World War II school to its present status of a highly attractive, on-the-move college with wait-lists of prospective students anxious to attend.

In my time associated with Saint Michael's College there has been a remarkable expansion of the notable extracurricular activities. I hesitate to be specific here, lest I omit any deserving mention, but some that immediately come to mind are the Fire and Rescue Squads that serve so nobly not only the Saint Michael's Campus but also the surrounding communities. Edmundite Campus Ministry—so essential to the College's mission—has continuously expanded its program and outreach over the years. One of these programs, MOVE (Mobilization of Volunteer Efforts), has received much well deserved recognition for its encouragement of volunteerism among Saint Michael's students, faculty, and staff. There is now an outstanding Wilderness Program with a full-time director offering a wide variety of opportunities for students to enjoy and develop outdoor skills, so appealing in Vermont. The popular Study Abroad programs enable Saint Michael's students to prepare for and contribute to the multicultural world they will soon encounter.

◆ (facing page) Each Miketown apartment had three large rooms and all of the apartments were fully furnished, including a refrigerator and an electric stove. "It isn't an uncommon sight now during the day here at Saint Mike's to see many proud mothers wheeling their offspring around the campus while Daddy is at class" (1950 yearbook). Pictured here, a father kisses his son on commencement day. ◆ (above) Registration for Saint Michael's AFROTC program began the week of September 29, 1951. Very quickly, over 200 Michaelmen signed up. Pictured here is James F. McDonald '54 at an AFROTC ceremony held in 1953. ◆ (below) The Air Force ROTC program began in September 1951. Sixty-two out of 450 colleges were selected for the program. AFROTC students took the same courses as other Saint Michael's students, but were also required to take specific AFROTC courses and drills from Air Force personnel.

Athletics also continue to enjoy growth and success at the College; for example, we now have not only a men's varsity hockey team, but also a women's varsity hockey team! There is little, if any, excuse for a student to be a "couch potato."

The Saint Michael's College of 1947-1951 was for me a wonderful gift and opportunity to grow spiritually, academically and intellectually, and introduced me to both the Edmundites and some exceptional teachers and human beings among the faculty and staff. I also made a lasting friendship with fellow students. For all this I am forever grateful. At the same time, I know that the contemporary Saint Michael's College has even more to offer today's students.

With the drastic downturn in religious vocations, there is no longer a long line of Edmundites on campus processing to their evening prayer in the College chapel, as there was in my undergraduate years. There is no longer an Edmundite as College president or chair of the board, or even heading up the dean's offices. The president is now a layperson, as is the academic dean and the dean of students. These changes are signs of the times, but not necessarily bad signs. Saint Michael's has received excellent administrative leadership from the laity who are conscientious in trying to maintain and enhance the Catholic and Edmundite heritage of the College.

Finally, I would be remiss, I think, if I did not mention the Saint Michael's presidents over these 55 years, up to and including the present, both Edmundites and laymen (no women – yet). They have been exceptional people who have given and do give the College outstanding visionary leadership. I expect that those previous presidents, whom I did not know, did the same. ◆

◆ Members of the Society of Saint Edmund at Saint Michael's College in 1954-1955. This year also marked the celebration of the College's fiftieth anniversary. (Front row): Reverend Ralph Linnehan, Reverend Daniel Lyons, Reverend John Herrouet, Reverend Eugene Alliot, Reverend Lorenzo D'Agostino, Very Reverend Francis Moriarty, Reverend Gerald Dupont, Reverend Vincent Maloney, Reverend Gerard Duford, Reverend Edmund Hamel. (Middle row): Brother Charles Gilson, Reverend John Stankiewicz, Reverend Adrien St. Charles, Reverend Armand Dubé, Reverend T. Donald Sullivan, Reverend John Lanoue, Reverend Maurice Boucher, Reverend Raymond Poirier, Reverend Leon Paulin. (Back row): Brother Arthur Breen, Brother Bernard Wood, Brother Paul Pinard, Brother Josaphat Brault, Reverend James Coombs, Brother Romuald Therrien, Brother Leo Duford, Brother Anthony Krutch, Reverend John Crowley, Reverend Paul Gopaul.

◆ (above) Dedication of Alumni Hall, July 21, 1956: Alumni Hall was named for the alumni of the College who directed their contributions for the building's construction in 1955. Alumni was the second of the four quadrangle dormitories to be built. The remaining two were completed in 1960 and 1961 respectively. ◆ (bottom left) In October 1956, Hungary was invaded and overtaken by Soviet troops and tanks. The United States agreed to accept 188,000 refugees and in January 1957, 101 Hungarian Freedom Fighters arrived in Vermont. Many were students who had been studying at the University of Budapest and were quickly integrated into Saint Michael's College's academic program. Each Hungarian student was teamed with a Saint Michael's student and began to learn English. This was the largest number of refugees ever integrated into a college program in the United States. ◆ (bottom right) The Alliot Student Center was constructed in 1959 and named in honor of College founder and fifth president Reverend Eugene Alliot, SSE, who served as president from 1908 until 1919. When told the building, which contained a new dining hall, would be named in his honor, Reverend Alliot laughed and remarked, "They will still call it the Chow Hall." The $1 million building was dedicated in 1960, when this photo was taken.

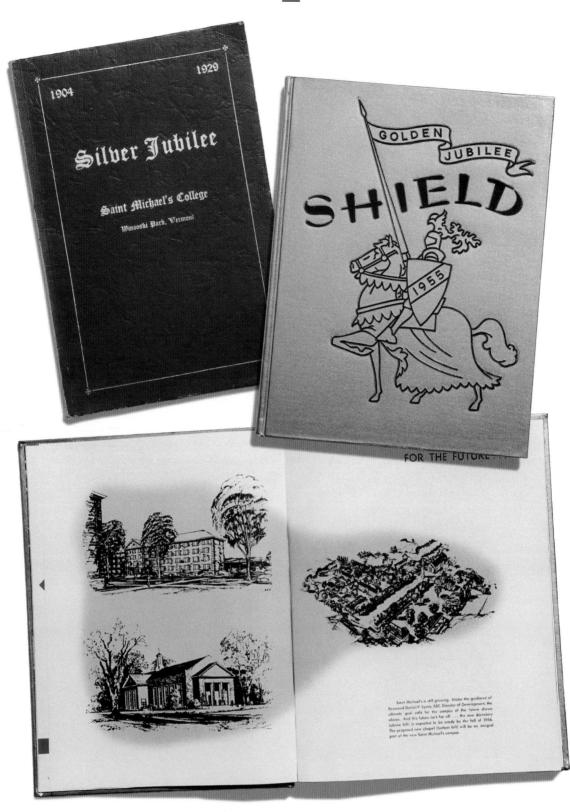

◆ (above left) Saint Michael's celebrated its twenty-fifth anniversary in 1929 with a special *Book of Reminiscences of Saint Michael's College*. The celebration was dedicated to the memory of Very Reverend Amand Prével, SSE. ◆ (above right) In 1955 Saint Michael's celebrated its fiftieth anniversary. The *Shield* printed a special cover to celebrate and a publication, *Saint Michael's Through the Years*, was written by Reverend Vincent B. Maloney, SSE, and Jeremiah K. Durick '23. ◆ (below) "Plan for the Future" from the Jubilee *Shield*: The administration of the College remained committed to looking at the future at the fiftieth anniversary mark. A development plan was widely circulated on campus and printed in numerous publications including the *Shield* and *The Michaelman*.

◆ (above) A ten-year development plan was unveiled by President Gerald Dupont in October 1959. The plan set a goal of raising $2,500,000 for growth, physical plant expansion and academic advances. ◆ (below) In September 1964, the College acquired approximately 130 acres and thirty buildings at the former Ethan Allen Air Base. The property had been declared surplus by the federal government and a large portion was deeded to Saint Michael's. The acquisition included the Ethan Allen Apartments; four classroom buildings; a dormitory; a post office; theater and chapel; a gymnasium; the former base headquarters and four major service buildings.

Paul Talley

◆ (above) Chapel of Saint Michael the Archangel ◆ (below left)
The *Saint Michael Review* celebrates the chapel groundbreaking ◆
(below right) Bishop Robert Joyce of Burlington consecrated the
Chapel of Saint Michael the Archangel in July of 1965. The house of
worship was dedicated to the clergy of the Diocese of Burlington.

◆ (left) Girls at Saint Michael's? In April 1970, the Board of Trustees approved a proposal by President Bernard Boutin to become a co-educational institution. Some concern was voiced over breaking the long established all-male tradition, which culminated in trustee Richard Coffey placing an ad in the New England edition of *Time* magazine promoting the move. "We've always been a quasi-co-educational school," said President Boutin, because for many years Saint Michael's hosted female students from Fanny Allen, Trinity College and Jeanne Mance School of Nursing. ◆ (below) "We arrived. Seventeen of us. Directed to the building in which we would live, isolated way out there on the North Campus," recalled Louise Stafford '72. Stafford was one of the first four female graduates of the College and is seen here crossing the dais. While a student at the College, she served as the first female editor of *The Michaelman*.

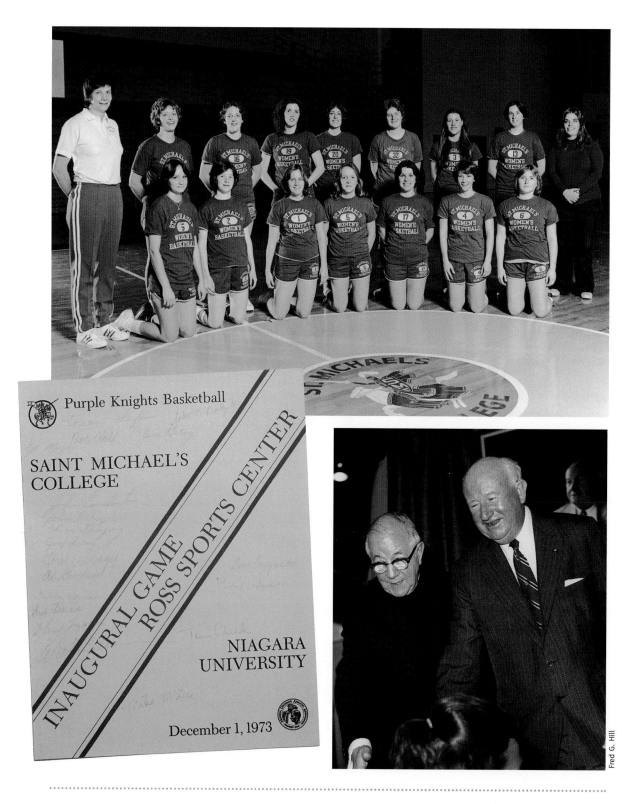

Fred G. Hill

◆ (above) 1976-77 Woman's Basketball Team ◆ (below) The inaugural game at Ross Sports Center was played against Niagara University on December 1, 1973. In 1971, Prentice Hall publisher and College trustee Vincent C. Ross gifted the College $500,000 for the construction of an athletic facility. His gift was part of the $8.5 million Promise for Tomorrow campaign undertaken by the College under the direction of President Bernard L. Boutin. Reverend Jeremiah Purtill, SSE '29, and Vincent Ross both attended the dedication of the Vincent C. Ross Sports Center in 1973.

◆ (above) The George D. Aiken Plaza was situated adjacent to Jeanmarie Hall, on the site where Austin Hall had stood for many years. Dedicated to Vermont's Senator Aiken on May 1, 1971, the Aiken Mall included a 2,204-square-foot park with maple trees. Saint Edmund's Hall now stands on this site. ◆ (below) The Society of Saint Edmund at the 1974 General Chapter. Front row: Raymond Doherty, '51, James Sullivan '23, Richard Myhalyk '67, Leon Paulin '37, Joseph Hart '51, Francis Moriarty '40, Eymard Galligan '43, Jeremiah Purtill '29, Francis Gokey '51, John Casey '34, Aime Trahan '34 John Stankiewicz '37, and Paul Hebert '37. Second row: Richard Page '72, Richard Berube '66, Stephen Hornat '72, J. Lawrence Ouimet '70, Paul McQuillen '72, James McKearin '67, Lorenzo D'Agostino '38, Kevin Callahan '73, Raymond Poirier '70, George Valley '77, Henry Nadeau, Charles Noel '34, T. Donald Sullivan '34, Charles Many '70, Charles Ranges '67, and Fred McLachlan '60. Back row: Martin Slattery, Gerald Grace '51, Howard Muehlberger '67, Philippe Simonnet, Paul Morin '36, Charles McNeice '58, Henry Albiser '40, Edward Conlin '41, Ernest Simard '40, John Crowley '71, Casmir Cichanowicz '39, James Robinson '53, (down) Oliva Langlois '33, (up) Edward Leary '46, (down) Ralph Linnehan '21, (up) Robert Sheehey '39, (down) John Chevalier '42, Russ Wise '59, (down) James Holden '59, (down) Jeffrey Archambeault '77, (up) David Bryan '63, (down) Thomas Berube '77, and John Meagher '62.

◆ (top left) The promotional poster for *The Glass Menagerie*, the dedication play in the McCarthy Arts Center. ◆ (top right) On August 1, 1975, Joanne Rathgeb, professor of fine arts, pictured left, and a talented cast, presented the dedication play *The Glass Menagerie* at the McCarthy Arts Center. ◆ (below) As a result of the successful Promise for Tomorrow campaign, the Michael & Margaret McCarthy Arts Center was dedicated on August 1, 1975 in honor of the McCarthy's, honorary degree recipients and benefactors, pictured here with President Reverend Moriarty, SSE.

◆ (above) Aerial view of Saint Michael's campus in the 1950s ◆ (below)   ◆ (following pages) Aerial view of Saint Michael's campus in the 1990s
Aerial view of Saint Michael's campus in the 1980s

◆ (above) Paul J. Reiss, pictured here in 1993 talking with the Most Reverend Moses B. Anderson, SSE '54, auxiliary bishop of Detroit, was inaugurated as the fourteenth president of Saint Michael's College in 1985 and served for ten years. ◆ (below left) President Bernard Boutin, Saint Michael's first lay president, was inaugurated in 1969. Bernard Boutin, the College's eleventh president, focused on fiscal management during his tenure. ◆ (below right) Rich Tarrant '65 at the dedication of the Jeremiah J. and Kathleen C. Tarrant Student Recreation Center in 1994. The Tarrant Center offers a variety of recreational opportunities that complement those available in the attached Ross Sports Center.

Paul Talley

◆ (above) Named for the patron saint of the Edmundite community, Saint Edmund's Hall was constructed between 1986 and 1987. The new building provided additional classrooms and much needed faculty offices. ◆ (below) Present-day Saint Edmund's Hall.

IDENTITY

John Peter Kenney, *Dean of the College*

A college is a community of readers. That is its literal meaning and its most fundamental intent. It is a gathering of master readers, sought out by those who hope to acquire the ways and means of learning, and surrounded by others who support and amplify that project. While a college may seem to be many things and to promise even more, it is this community of scholars, dedicated to the pursuit of knowledge and the presence of truth, that is its core.

And that is in essence what we do here on this hilltop above Lake Champlain in northern Vermont.

We are a society that theorizes and experiments, ponders and discusses. We do this because we share in the universal human desire to give meaning to the life in which we find ourselves, hostages as we are to time, in a world not of our making. We do so because we trust that we can figure things out, and discover truth.

Les Pères de Pontigny, our founders, were foreigners and fugitives to this frigid and unpromising land. They came, of course, not to engage in disinterested inquiry but to preserve the Catholic cause and to instill its ancient modes of learning among the young in North America. Heavens knows what they were

◆ (facing page) In 1984, fifty-one Japanese girls from Seibo Junior High School arrived at Saint Michael's. They were the first group to study English under an agreement between Saint Michael's and another institution. Today, the College has similar agreements with many institutions across the world. ◆ (above) Jeanmarie Hall, named for the College's fourth president, stands alongside Route 15 as a symbol of the College's academic identity.

thinking. But they stayed and young Americans came, as they still do, long after the founders have passed on and the urgency of their immediate purpose has dissipated. Yet something of that original intent remains. For the Edmundites studied and taught within a tradition, and their learning was that of the Catholic Church, itself the founder of the European university system. Indeed they took their name from a saint who was the first doctor of divinity to teach in Oxford, at the nascence of the college system in England. While the political struggle that sent them into exile has long since been consigned to the history of old Europe, some of the force of their project remains: to offer an education grounded in Catholic learning. While our work today goes beyond that purpose, it still proceeds from it.

We can thus find in our origins some clues to our present identity. We are a Catholic college and, moreover, we are an American one. The American part is easy to see in this book's photographs. Saint Michael's was a college for Catholic immigrants to America. The French Edmundites were not so much immigrants as expatriates on loan; indeed some returned eventually to France and are buried in the crypt at Pontigny. They were here in America for a reason, but they were not really participants in the American experiment. Yet their students were enthusiastic recruits to Jefferson's new race of democratic Americans. They were Catholics in Protestant New England, from families of recent arrival, but they intended to be citizens of this new land. And that is why they were at Saint Michael's – to get an education and get a start. They were part of the promise of America in the twentieth century, the promise of economic prosperity, political liberty and religious tolerance. Of course they were at Saint Michael's because some of these promises were as yet realized. Immigrants from French Canada, Ireland, Italy, or

◆ The sight of the bell tower atop Founders Hall evokes pleasant memories for graduates of any decade. This illustration was painted by Ed Diemand '47, editor of the first *Shield*. ◆ (facing page) A simple metal sign marked the College along a snow-covered Route 15.

Poland were not highly regarded in Yankee society and places in Protestant colleges were largely unavailable to them. And so for several generations in the last century Saint Michael's was a Catholic college by default—a place where immigrants could go for a higher education. That is the paradox of our early identity: we were a Catholic college run by French priests for immigrants who wanted to become more American without losing their souls. Somehow it seems to have worked.

You can also see another American collegiate feature in these pictures: that the Michaelmen of yore were having some fun. That too seems to have been a Winooski Park tradition from the early days. It may not have been written into the mission of the College, but it has long been part of our American identity. Whatever else can be said of our noble clerical founders, a zest for good times was probably not central to their charism. But the students at their immigrant college found ways to interpolate good cheer into the gravitas of French Catholicism. One might even view this as a sign of spiritual confidence,

if one insists. Coeducation seems to have both tempered and embellished this trajectory of collegiate levity. And so to the despair of many administrators, present and past, Saint Michael's established a well-deserved reputation as a fun place to go to college.

So it can be said that our identity is at least this: we are a college within the Catholic community in America. That is broadly a sociological characterization of Saint Michael's. To get at the deeper question of our identity as a Catholic college we must step back and consider the central characteristic of the Catholic intellectual tradition: its commitment to the pursuit of wisdom and truth. This is sometimes viewed these days as a hopelessly outdated quest, in an academic environment often characterized by soft relativism in the humanities and utilitarianism in the sciences. But that is what we are still after here at Saint Michael's – Truth with a capital T. Catholicism is based on a faith in the intelligibility of reality, on the belief that reality is rationally grounded. What we seek to know is the nature of things as they truly are, and the wisdom to value them accordingly. So our purpose is to

discover the deep structures of knowledge that lead to wisdom, not just the surface patterns that allow us to manipulate nature for profit. And so it is also our goal to discover and teach the enduring values that proceed from an understanding of things as they are. We believe that truth does indeed yield to human inquiry, and that it can set us free.

The importance of this moral intention in education is perhaps best exhibited in one chapter in the larger history of the College, one that draws together the Catholic and the American identities of Saint Michael's. I have in mind the courageous involvement of Father Maurice Ouellette and the Edmundites in the Civil Rights struggle of the 1960s. When Martin Luther King Jr. wrote his famous letter from the jailhouse in Birmingham, Alabama, he appealed to the natural rights of all human beings, to their God-given dignity beneath the established laws of any

....

◆ (facing page) Unidentified students read a newspaper outside College (now Jeanmarie) Hall. ◆ (below) The Sisters of Saint Martha arrived at Saint Michael's College in 1933 and took charge of many of the domestic duties. They served at Saint Michael's for thirty years.

society that may, in fact, trammel upon that human dignity. For King those fundamental rights were based on the nature of the human person as a creature of God. This type of thinking harks all the way back to Justice McLean's dissenting opinion in the Dred Scott case, in which he decried the view that a black man should be viewed only as chattel: "He bears the impress of his Maker, and is amenable to the laws of God and man; and he is destined to an endless existence." For the Edmundites, schooled in classical Catholic ethics, the moral logic of this appeal was compelling, for it asserted truths that went beyond mere politics. These were moral claims that had a foundation in what they had come to know—through their education and their lives—to be true and real.

Something of the Edmundite response in this historical instance is at the heart of the Catholic mission of Saint Michael's College. It is not easy to characterize. But there is a moral seriousness about our project, rooted in our conviction that we do indeed bear the impress of a Creator, that there are rational

patterns to be discovered through our intellectual labors, that we are ennobled by the promise of an eternal destiny. These are the first things about which we must be serious, the things that really matter. Because we think like this at the core of our Catholic tradition, we can accord to others the intellectual freedom to think as they wish and to disagree with our positions, as long as they too are honest and serious and respectful of the rights of all interlocutors. Our respect for the truth makes us open to all who seek it and even to those who are unsure that it can be found.

This pursuit of truth in the Catholic liberal arts tradition thus represents an intensification of the best in the contemporary academy. It is the ennobling ingredient that has retained the moral significance of scholarship and learning. It rescues higher education from being reduced to a merely social role, as an expensive rite of passage or an introduction to the upper class. This Catholic commitment to foundational truth is a point of renewed salience in our academic culture. That remains the special promise of Saint Michael's College and the core of our identity as we enter our second century. ◆

◆ (above) In 1963, the nuns of the Sisters of Saint Martha returned to Canada. Their recall to the Mother House left an immense void, as they prepared every meal and were in charge of the college laundry.

◆ (facing page) Reverend Paul Morin, SSE '36, speaks with a student's family in 1960 near Cheray Science Hall (left) and Jeanmarie Hall.

◆ (above) Initially envisioned by Reverend Arthur Rivard, SSE, a physics professor, it was James M. Holcomb who put much effort into the creation of an observatory. Holcomb, an expert lens maker and former math professor, oversaw the construction of the observatory and built the original mounting for the telescope. The Holcomb Observatory has stood across Route 15 since 1939. ◆ (below) Students crowd around the mail room window in hopes of finding a package from home. ◆ (facing page above) Student members of Knights of the Altar kneel in the Jeanmarie chapel in 1962. Knights of the Altar was founded in 1958 to help with the implementation of the College's spiritual program under the moderation of Reverend Nelson Ziter, SSE '43. Students in the group served at Mass, showed films about mission work and worked to promote the Catholic nature of Saint Michael's. ◆ (facing page center) Homecoming is celebrated annually by the Saint Michael's community. In 1951, the residents of Saint James Hall in "Miketown" won the homecoming prize of fifteen dollars with their creation, "The Castle." ◆ (facing page below) Saint Michael's is surrounded by the Green Mountains. Vermont's highest peak, Mount Mansfield, can be easily seen to the east on clear, sunny days.

◆ (above) A group of unidentified Michaelmen in 1954. ◆ (below right) Reverend Ray Doherty, SSE '51, was director of campus ministry and an admissions officer for many years. He continues to be an enduring presence on campus. Father Ray, as he is known, has a knack for remembering the names of every student he has ever met. ◆ (facing page) Three Michaelmen pass by Cheray (right) and Jeanmarie (left) with books in hand during a winter in the 1960s.

Harry R. Stevens

Robert Hagerman

◆ (facing page) Seal featuring Saint Michael on top of Jeanmarie Hall ◆ (above) The Saint Michael's community has always been strong, in part because of close-knit residential living. Here, students study in their Saint Joseph's Hall room. ◆ (below) When William

Rooney '60 and Thomas Purcell, Jr. '60 graduated in 1960, only three of the four quadrangle dormitories had been constructed. As seniors, they called Alumni Hall home.

◆ (facing page) A view from the green shows the Dupont Cross and the Chapel of Saint Michael the Archangel set against a Vermont sky.

◆ (above) Some of the first female students enrolled at the College.

◆ (below) William Tortolano began as head of the music department in 1960. Prior to Saint Michael's admitting women, Tortolano conducted all-male choirs. Co-education brought with it more musical opportunities for the College chorale.

Nathan Bilow

◆ (above) Tricia Byrnes '98 was one of six United States female athletes to compete in the snowboard halfpipe event at the 2002 Olympic Games. She placed sixth overall. ◆ (below left) Students from the past several decades have enjoyed working with Jennifer Cernosia, assistant dean of students and director of student activities. Jennie's office has long been a comfortable space for any student to spend some time. ◆ (below right) In the early 1980s, the College commissioned and purchased its first mascot costume. The mascot, a soft, furry, purple creature with a gold knight's helmet atop its head, lasted about a decade. The mascot is pictured here with Kim Palmese '84 and Judy Fischer '84 in 1984.

SAINT MICHAEL'S COLLEGE
Athletic Logos (1904 – present)

Navy Logo 1907 – 1912

Purple Knight 1st version

Navy Logo 1913 – 1919

Purple Knight 2nd version

ST. M

SAINT M

M

1920 – 1935

1947 – 1998

1998 – 1999

Current Alternate Logo

Current Main Logo

SAINT MICHAEL'S COLLEGE
Academic Seals (1904 – present)

1905

1907

1907 alternate

1914

1930s

1948

1970s – 1980s

1980s – 1990s

Current Seal

COMMUNITY

Senator Patrick Leahy '61

I sometimes wonder if the small group of Edmundites who emigrated from France and Canada to what is now Colchester had any idea about the impact their selfless acts would have on the culture and community surrounding the farmhouse where Saint Michael's College began. French Canadians, as my wife Marcelle will affirm, are known for their strong wills and independent-mindedness. And these attributes, thanks to the work of the Edmundites, have helped shape Chittenden County, Vermont, and, in a subtle way, the entire nation.

Despite what my grandson may think, it was not quite back in the age of dinosaurs that I graduated from Saint Michael's, in 1961. Governor F. Ray Keyser Jr. was in the statehouse. Mayor John Lockhart was finishing his tenure as mayor of Burlington. It would be another two years before the winds of change put the first Democrat since the Civil War into the Vermont governorship—my friend Governor Phillip Hoff.

Today, Marcelle and I still walk by the parts of the campus where we dated decades ago—and where she and her fellow nurses went to classes. The campus

◆ (facing page) Founders Hall in Autumn ◆ (below) Students congregate at the intersection of Route 15 and Lime Kiln Road in the 1940s. Greystone Hall, now called Senior Hall, can be seen on the right. Old Hall, now known as Founders Hall, is to the left through the trees. Today this is a busy intersection.

has changed dramatically. And as the campus has changed, so has the State of Vermont. But one thing has remained constant—the caliber of the Saint Michael's graduate and his or her effect on the state we live in.

My classmates were good people. Like most Michaelmen, we were often off campus and over in Winooski, Essex Junction and Colchester, giving our time to those needing some help, in the same spirit in which the Edmundites gave their time—and their lives—to those who needed it more than a century ago. Like the Edmundites, Saint Michael's students are invited to be part of something greater than ourselves, and to give back through service to others. Today, whenever I visit my alma mater, I am continually impressed and encouraged by how this spirit has endured. I am constantly reading in the local newspapers about Saint Michael's students traveling to Alabama, Africa or Baltimore to help youngsters and families in need. My office regularly receives resolutions

from the school's student government, advocating on behalf of issues of global concern.

Since its humble and inspirational beginnings, Saint Michael's has been a service-driven experience. Its graduates are well-educated, complete human beings, and Vermont is a better place for it. Perhaps this is best exemplified by the programs that reach into Vermont's communities sponsored by the Mobilization of Volunteer Efforts (MOVE) office or by our campus ministry program. Students from the MOVE program play volleyball with inmates from the local correctional facility, go to dances with senior citizens, and mentor local youths. Our campus ministry program, as it has for a long time, serves not only Saint Michael's students, but also hundreds of

◆ (above) Members of the community deposit mail into the US Postal Service box near Founders Hall in the 1940s. The College's mailroom was housed in Founders Hall and later Jeanmarie Hall. Today the community's mail is delivered to and distributed in the basement of Joyce Hall.

local families. We have a fire department and an ambulance service that daily reaches out as far as Hinesburg, and on some occasions, they drive as far as Boston to transport premature babies. One of my more recent memories of Saint Michael's is falling from about 12,000 feet above the Champlain Valley Fair Grounds with the Army Golden Knights parachute team and watching a small white ambulance on the ground loom larger and larger. Only after I landed did I notice it was the young men and women of Saint Michael's College standing by with their ambulance. Thankfully, I did not need to use their services.

Through the construction of landmarks like the Ross Sports Center, the McCarthy Arts Center, the Chapel of Saint Michael the Archangel and many other facilities, the Edmundites, Michaelmen and Purple Knights who lead our school have turned the former Kelly farm into an enclave of Vermont culture

....

◆ (below) Students relaxing in the basement of Ryan Hall, Recreation/Lounge Area, circa early 1960s.

—a place where Vermonters travel distances short and long to visit, to catch a concert, to hear a speaker or to cheer for the home team.

Increasingly, the spirit of Saint Michael's is expanding wider and wider off campus as the school becomes not only a part of the community but also a cornerstone of the community. At the Firehouse Gallery on Church Street in downtown Burlington, or at ECHO at the Leahy Center for Lake Champlain, Saint Michael's gives to the community what an institution of higher education should give. And the spirit of Vermont is likewise felt on campus. The Vermont Youth Orchestra practices on our campus. Members of the Vermont National Guard use our gyms. Vermonters have access to an expanding resource within the Durick Library.

It is difficult to find a Vermonter without a connection to Saint Michael's. So often, as I travel throughout the state, Vermonters who know my association with Saint Michael's tell me about their siblings or children who went there. More often, I hear about the many accomplishments of the school's

graduates in business, in public service, in medicine and so many other fields.

My Michaelman roots run thick through my bones. My time on campus was instrumental to my understanding of the world, and of myself. I am grateful for the experience, and I am grateful that Vermont and Saint Michael's College have each other.

Our Edmundites, our professors, our staff and our students have profoundly shaped Vermont for the past 100 years. And I predict we will do so for the next 100 years. ◆

◆ (above) Joyce Hall, named after Bishop Robert Joyce, bishop of Burlington, was constructed in 1961, completing the fourth quadrangle dormitory. ◆ (below) Upon their arrival at Saint Michael's, students quickly became aware of the advantages and disadvantages of residential dormitory living. In 1957, men in Alumni Hall share a bathroom to prepare for a big night out.

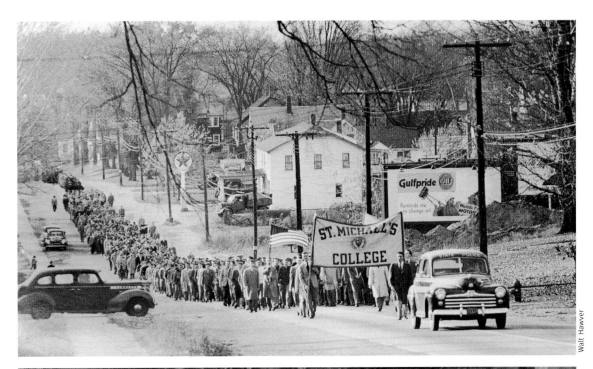

Walt Hawver

◆ (above) In October 1948, Saint Michael's students participated in a parade from Winooski's bridge to Saint Michael's College in honor of the statue of Our Lady of Fatima. Following the parade, the statue was placed in shrine in Austin Hall. The Trapp Family Singers provided choral music at the services, and over 1,000 people participated.

◆ (below) During the "Iron Knights" years, there was great community support for Doc Jacobs' Knights. In 1957, the basketball team once again traveled to Evansville, Indiana, for the national basketball finals. Hotel Vermont in downtown Burlington proudly displayed its support of the team.

◆ (above) Maureen McNamara, pictured here with Thomas Garrett, spent many years in service to the Saint Michael's community as Registrar, as well as coordinating extension services, graduate programs and the TESL program. ◆ (below left) Ann Marie Leggett, "The Voice of Saint Michael's," began working at the College as a French-speaking young woman of seventeen. She retired in 2000 after working in the mailroom and as the switchboard operator for fifty-one years. ◆ (below right) For many years, Jane Campbell headed up health services and was a well-known face on campus.

Rob Swanson

◆ (above) Dorothy Williams, former director of Multicultural Student Affairs, speaking at the College's Martin Luther King Jr. Convocation. This event, held yearly and sponsored by the Office of Multicultural Student Affairs and the MLK Society, brings renowned speakers to the College to speak on issues of race, tolerance and diversity. ◆ (below) Although Saint Michael's is no longer officially located in the city of Winooski (a change in postal regulations now has the campus' address in Colchester), many students over the years have become very familiar with the small city's downtown area. "The Mill" was, for several decades, the prime hangout for Saint Michael's students. Today, Winooski's Higher Ground draws many students for its live music.

John McKeith

Ken Burris

Carolyn Bates

◆ (above) Dormitory in the winter ◆ (below left) In 1996, the Wilderness Program was launched and provides outdoor adventure programs throughout the year for students with various interests and abilities. Students are taught leadership skills through explorations and adventures in Vermont's vast wilderness. ◆ (below right) Radio at Saint Michael's dates back to the mid-1950s with WSSE. The station operated on an AM frequency which ran through an electrical current in the dormitories. In the 1960s, the College obtained a noncommercial educational FM license from the FCC and the station's call letters were changed to WWPV. The station remains student-run, although since 1998 Vermont Public Radio has been allotted some airtime for its international programming. ◆ (facing page above left) The Office of Multicultural Student Affairs provides students of all races and cultures the opportunity to come together for dialogue and solidarity. Students who work in the office, and the clubs associated with it, plan various events throughout the year associated with diversity and acceptance. ◆ (facing page above right) Minutes from beautiful Lake Champlain, Saint Michael's students frequent the waterfront for studying, quiet reflection and relaxation. ◆ (facing page below) At Saint Michael's, students live together, learn together and grow together. Varying residential options provide students with the ability to choose a housing option that best fits their needs.

John McKeith

Paul Talley

John McKeith

Sanders Milens

◆ (above) In 1970, Don Sutton, dean of students, together with Tom Powers '70 and Peter Maloska '71, helped establish the Saint Michael's College Volunteer Fire and Rescue Department. The Fire and Rescue squad members are pictured here in 1975. ◆ (below) Houses along College Parkway have been used as student residences since the 1970s. In recent years, students wishing to live in the houses must present a programmatic theme for their residence, and those chosen for theme houses must demonstrate commitment to their theme throughout the year. Jay Foley, Tom Katkus, Dave Shiveley, Dave Ondrusek, and Roy Carcia are pictured at 92 College Parkway in 1977.

◆ (above) Since their construction, the Quad dorms of Joyce, Ryan, Lyons and Alumni have been home to most students during their time at Saint Michael's. ◆ (below) In 1994, members of the Saint Michael's community teamed up for a basketball challenge. The faculty and staff team included (back row) Mike Samara, Patrick Gallivan '89, Jeff Adams, Reverend Mike Cronogue, SSE, Robert Kenney, Steve McMahon and Major Brian Chaisson. (front row) Zafir Bludevich, Jerry Flanagan '71 and President Paul Reiss.

John McKeith

John McKeith

John McKeith

◆ (facing page) The College's commitment to being almost 100 percent residential allows for community building and interaction to occur every day. Here, students from Lyons Hall embark on a day of downhill skiing while building friendships that may last a lifetime. ◆ (above) Saint Michael's Fire and Rescue squads respond to more than 300 fire and 2,000 rescue calls annually from the four commu-

nities and Route 15 corridor that they serve. Forty students and twelve alumni volunteer on the squads. ◆ (below) Danielle Simmer '03 works with children through one of MOVE's many volunteer programs. The After School Games Program allows volunteers to become role models for area children by participating in activities at the Burlington Boys' and Girls' Club.

Ken Burris

Owen Stayner

◆ (above) The Chapel of Saint Michael the Archangel serves as a house of worship for college students and local residents. The chapel is also used for many special services, including the yearly sacred tradition of Lessons & Carols, which features performances by the College Choral and Wind Ensemble as well as scripture readings by members of the Saint Michael's community. ◆ (below) MOVE (Mobilization of Volunteer Efforts) was founded in 1988 and has grown tremendously since then. Seventy percent of Saint Michael's students participate in a MOVE program at least once during their time at the College. Here, volunteers work and form friendships with area senior citizens. The Senior Citizen Outreach Program strives to establish close, positive relationships with seniors who might otherwise be alone.

Buff Lindau

Paul Talley

◆ (above) An annual event, MOVE's Shack-A-Thon increases awareness around the issues of homelessness and raises money for the good works of Habitat for Humanity. ◆ (below) In 1983 Saint Michael's was awarded a cost-reduction incentive award because of its townhouse building program. Townhouses provide alternative housing arrangements for upper-level students. Most townhouses include single rooms, a kitchen and a common living room space.

Owen Stayner

◆ (previous page) The Church Street Marketplace of downtown Burlington is frequented by Saint Michael's students. The College's closeness to Vermont's largest city attracts many students to the area. ◆ (above) Saint Michael's is committed to maintaining the North Campus in the historic Fort Ethan Allen. Many students prefer North Campus because of its separation from Main Campus and the spacious rooms in many of the North Campus residence halls. ◆ (below) During his first days on campus, President vanderHeyden sought out numerous students for conversation. Miranda Brink '98, Andrew Hescock '97, Tracey Stevens '00 and Erin Kluis '99 share their views with him in the Emmaus Courtyard.

Ken Burris

Alden Pellett

◆ (above) When warm spring air arrives and the snow finishes melting, students flock to the green between the Chapel and the library where they relax and enjoy the beginning of the beautiful spring season. ◆ (below left) Students enjoy an afternoon in downtown Burlington at the Church Street Marketplace. Besides featuring many small shops and restaurants, Church Street is home to the newly renovated Burlington Town Center, Vermont's only two-level shopping mall. ◆ (below right) Reverend Michael P. Cronogue, SSE, pauses in an Alliot Hall stairwell to speak with several students. Father Mike, a 20-year veteran of the College and former director of campus ministry, established the Edmundite Center for Peace and Justice in 1999, whose mission is "to integrate peace and justice concerns into the everyday life of our college community."

EDUCATION OF THE HUMAN PERSON

Susan W. Kuntz, *Professor of Psychology*

A few years ago, when a reporter asked what Saint Michael's College meant to me, I responded: "It's a place to find your soul." I meant, then as well as now, that Saint Michael's is a place where one is able to think, to explore the moral and emotional part of one's nature, to experience the inherent power of knowledge. A college, it seems to me, is where one connects with history, persons, places, objects, and life enhancing processes. It is where one takes in and transforms. "Education of the Human Person," the heart of Saint Michael's mission, implies personal depth, where one examines purpose and life and perhaps most importantly discovers the value of imagination, feelings, thoughts, sensations, and intuitions. Thomas Moore tells us the "soul is not a thing, but a quality or a dimension of experiencing life and ourselves." I think this an apt description of the education offered at this small Catholic college; it stays close to how

the soul is discovered as a vehicle of individual personal existence.

Although there are many parts to campus life, central to its being is the faculty, those deemed, rightly or wrongly, public intellectuals. Faculty members are bearers of critical knowledge, rules and values that

◆ Saint Michael's first course catalogue was printed in 1905. It is shown here along with the Centennial Catalogue of 2003-2005.

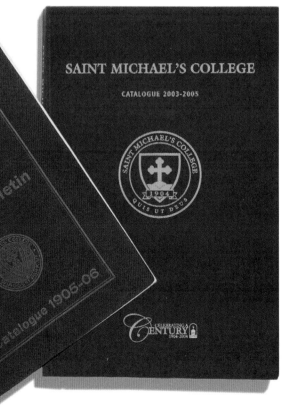

help us figure out the world in which we live. They articulate and problematize issues of importance to themselves, their colleagues and students, their areas of study and the wider community. This challenges the role of teacher as technician or public servant whose job it is to implement rather than conceptualize. I think the role of faculty is to legitimize campuses as places where people collectively struggle to understand the social, political and economic preconditions that make individual freedom and social empowerment possible. In this sense faculty roles are deeply imbued with moral and ethical implications. The classroom then becomes a space where they assert themselves as professional academics whose knowledge and action presuppose a vision of the educated person and the good life. The most important referent for this view of faculty, in my mind, rests in commitment, the promise to do well by the students, the institution, and by their discipline. Faculties are powerful forces both for preserving and spreading knowledge and

for producing it. In some ways this is a paradoxical situation. Faculty present truth as understood by themselves and others and at the same time challenge the suppositions upon which that truth is stated. Their efforts toward understanding are always contingent on the recognition that perspectives can be superceded, definitions of what it means to be educated can change, probably seen no more clearly than in changing curricular requirements and structures.

The most striking, and somewhat alarming (for those who study it) thing about curriculum is that debate and discussions never seem to get anywhere. I do not mean that decisions and policies are not arrived at and implemented; I mean there never seems to be an agreed advance in knowledge as an outcome of the talk. We are not able to say, "Well, at least we now know…" The many definitions given to curriculum suggest it is an eclectic framework consisting of learning opportunities, resources, and instructional strategies that empower students to

examine both the identity of the institution and their individual identities. At Saint Michael's, curriculum consists of requirements in the liberal arts and sciences which imply there is common knowledge necessary to be educated here—that of exposure to the humanities, philosophy and religion, social and natural sciences, classical and fine arts, language and cultural civilizations. There are also curriculum sequences particular to areas of study that compose what is known as the "major." Tension exists between these two strands of curriculum, and faculty debate the essentialness of some requirements that naturally detract from the resources given to others. This tension can be felt in

major areas of study as well, where faculty deliberate the level and breadth of experiences alongside notions of formality/informality and theoretical/applied. I see these tensions as healthy; they encourage examination both of what is being defined as knowledge and how the institution encourages students to explore it. Whatever curricular framework is used, the important point, it seems to me, is that every student has an opportunity to move deeper in their understanding of themselves and the world about them. We now live in a world subject to infinite interpretability, a culturally diverse society whose peoples do not know one another. The challenge to curricular structures is that they offer students ways to explore the complexities of their social and personal identities. Cultural connections are critical dimensions in the experience of the liberal arts where students grapple with multiplicity,

....

◆ (facing page) Students in the biology lab, 1937. ◆ (below) Students work in the third floor chemistry lab of College (Jeanmarie) Hall during the 1930s.

ambiguity, and difference as defining conditions in the contemporary world.

Although it is important that the curriculum reflect the richness and diversity of the students that attend the institution and exist in the world at large, it is also important to "de-center" the curriculum; that is, students need to be actively engaged in building their own learning. At Saint Michael's we sometimes introduce first-year students to academic life during orientation by asking them to read Plato's analogy of the cave, where they surmise that education's purpose is to lead people into the light, turning them from the world of appearance to the world of reality. A much less evident part of this text, at least to the students

Detore Photo Service

◆ (above) Librarian Reverend Vincent Maloney, SSE, assists Thomas McNamara '48 in the Founders Hall library during the 1948 academic year. The library was housed in Founders Hall until a surplus military building was brought from Fort Ethan Allen to serve as the new library. It became known as Klein Student Center in 1970. ◆ (below) Eighty Michaelmen and twelve women from Trinity College formed the Confraternity of Christian Doctrine group, which attended weekly classes held by Reverend Maurice Boucher, SSE. Every Sunday,

Michaelmen had the chance to apply their Catholic principles to the teaching of religious education to children in surrounding parishes. ◆ (facing page) Mid-year and final exams were the cause of much stress to Saint Michael's students. Exams were given in two-hour periods and were a winter and spring tradition. "We feared them, fought them, sweated them, studied for them, and most of us passed them...", wrote a *Shield* staff member in 1956.

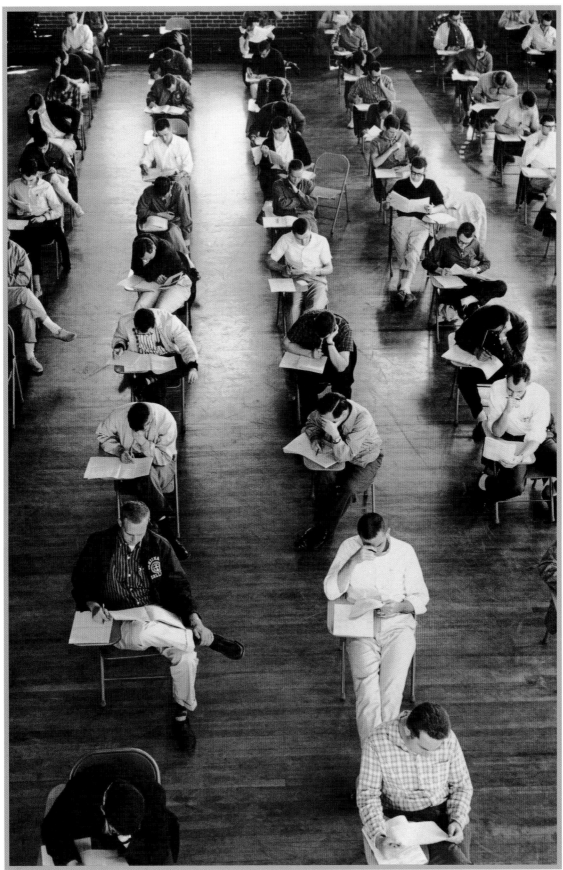

Robert Hagerman

with whom I have worked, is the idea that once one leaves the cave, there is an obligation to go back and participate in life there both by trying to understand the structure that is the cave and by developing compassion for those that reside there. I think all teachers in and beyond the classroom strive to make students agents of their own learning and instill in them returns to the cave. One vehicle where agency emerges most naturally, I offer, is from experiences and struggles found in "service learning" opportunities. This learning is distinguished from volunteer work and academic internships, although both beneficial in their own rights. Service learning is, according to Eyler and Giles (1999), "a form of experiential education where learning occurs through a cycle of action and reflec-

tion as students work with others through a process of applying what they are learning to community problems and at the same time reflecting upon their experiences as they seek to achieve new objectives with the community and deeper understanding and skills for themselves." The learning one does is recognized through curricular inclusion granting institutional credit not for the experience but for the learning that occurs as a result of the experience. Service learning activities are planned, intentional, and extend theoretical learning beyond the classroom so students can understand how social, political, and psychological constructs affect areas of life. Students develop habits of critical thinking and problem solving and learn to challenge authority systems that set up existing structures. Service learning is built on the premise that taking the classroom into the community improves both the classroom and the community, the infusion of both enhances student learning.

....

◆ (below) Edward F. Murphy taught English and humanities at the College during the 1950s and '60s. Besides his teaching duties, Murphy acted as moderator of the Debating Team, shown here in 1953. Club President John Carroll '54, right, looks on. ◆ (facing page) Reverend Lorenzo D'Agostino, SSE '38, instructing students in biology, circa 1950.

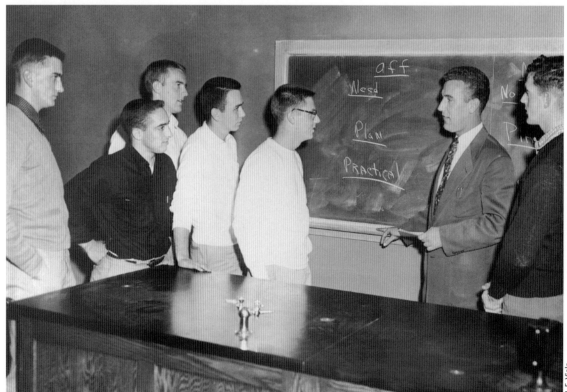

L.F. Viola

Reflecting today on the response I gave that reporter several years ago, I do believe that Saint Michael's is a place where faculty, students and curriculum interact in an attempt to understand and change the world. Working together one finds here, to rephrase Milton, "the hidden soul of harmony" in the guise of an educated person. I am inspired by the work of my colleagues and my students who strive for this utopian vision. A quote on my desk is a daily reminder of the importance of the work we do. It reads:

> Education is the point at which we decide whether we love the world enough to take responsibility for it and by the same token save it from ruin which except for renewal, except for the coming

of the new and young would be inevitable. And education, too, is where we decide whether we love our children enough not to expel them from our world and leave them to their own devices, not to strike from their hands their chance of undertaking something new, something unforeseen by us, but to prepare them in advance for the task of renewing a common world.

(Hannah Arendt, *Between Past and Future*)

The multi-layered meaning of Arendt's words reminds me that the notion of education is about responsibility, renewal, preparation and, ultimately, love. At Saint Michael's College I teach and learn to save my soul and those of my students. ◆

◆ (above left) John C. Hartnett '43, professor of biology, was awarded $1,900 by the American Cancer Society in 1963. The grant helped him to continue crucial research that he began while a doctoral candidate at the University of Vermont. ◆ (above right) Jeremiah K. Durick '23 was a foremost expert on Shakespeare and a beloved educator at Saint Michael's. As a poet, scholar, teacher and father, Durick exemplified the dedicated Catholic layman. He taught at Saint Michael's for 35 years. ◆ (below left) Reverend Edmund Hamel, SSE '17, was associated with Saint Michael's for over fifty years. He attended both the high school and college, then taught philosophy from 1923-1969. He also served as dean of men and dean of studies, and directed the College's first adult extension program. ◆ (below right) After serving in World War II, George A. Fortune '40 returned to Saint Michael's to teach elementary and advanced accounting for many years. He was one of the first professors at the College to be granted emeritus status.

◆ (above left) Edward L. Henry was Saint Michael's thirteenth president, serving from 1976 to 1985. Here, he stands with Vice President Walter Mondale, left, and Senator Patrick Leahy '61, right, during a September 1978 campus visit by Mondale. ◆ (above right) On May 16, 1954, John F. Kennedy, then a Junior Senator of Massachusetts, arrived at the College to speak at the annual rally of the Vermont State Holy Name Societies. He spoke to a large crowd on the topic of "Facing the Stern Encounter." ◆ (below) In 1963, Vice President Lyndon Johnson arrived at Saint Michael's to a crowd of 1,000. He told the crowd, "You are living in an exciting age...so make the most of it."

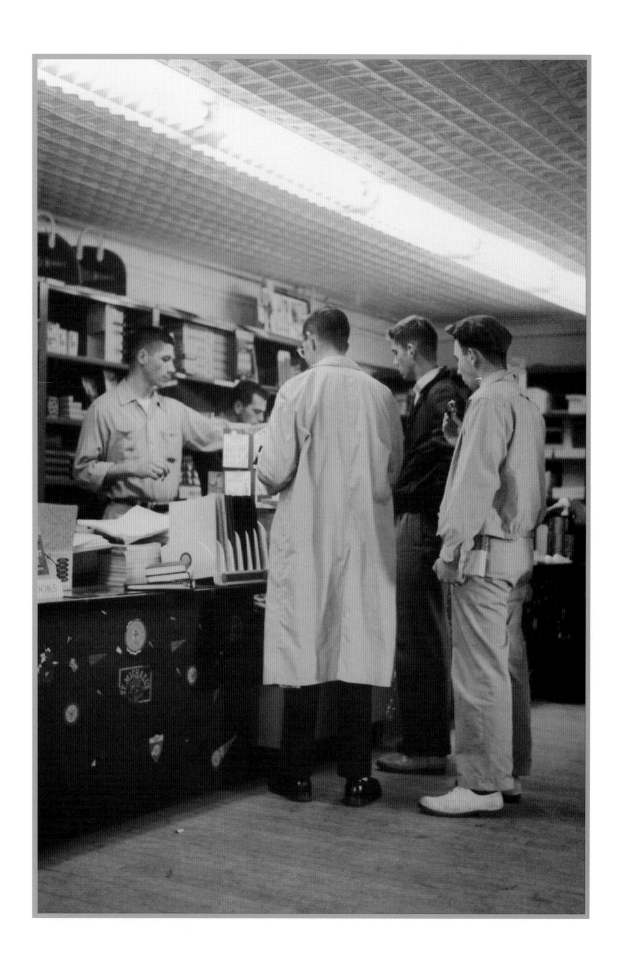

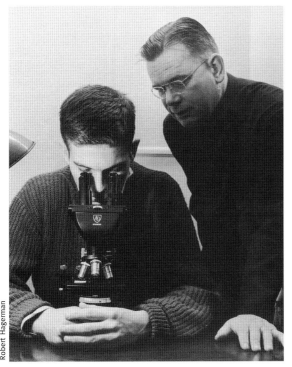

Robert Hagerman

◆ (facing page) The College's original bookstore was located in Founders Hall. ◆ (above) John D. Donoghue '32 was known by many as "Mr. Saint Michael's." He served as the College's first Public Relations and Sports Information Director from 1947-1966, and was successful in getting national exposure for the College. He also filled numerous other roles, including music director; professor of humanities, education, English, and journalism; associate trustee and chairman of the journalism department. He founded the College's first student newspaper, *The Michaelman*, and also oversaw production of the *Shield*. ◆ (below left) Reverend T. Donald Sullivan, SSE '34, returned to Saint Michael's in 1939 as an assistant professor of classical languages and then Dean of Studies. After earning his doctorate in cytogenetics he chaired the biology department and, in 1952, undertook a major cancer research project that brought the College nearly $10,000 in federal funds. "T.D." did not fully retire until 1982. ◆ (below right) Joseph Amrhein Jr. headed the Department of Business Administration and Accounting for a number of years.

Natalie Stultz

◆ (above) Reverend Gerald E. Dupont, SSE, pictured advising a student in the early 1950s, served as academic dean and then Saint Michael's tenth president from 1958 until 1969. ◆ (below left) Marie Henault, professor of English and humanities, became chair of the English department in 1969, the first woman to head a department at Saint Michael's. ◆ (below right) Henry G. Fairbanks led the humanities department, teaching English and the classics. ◆ (facing page) Dominique Casavant first came to Saint Michael's to pursue a master of the arts in philosophy, which he earned in 1955. An avid skier, Casavant coached Saint Michael's ski team, until 1960. In 1971, the same year he won the mayoral race in Winooski, Casavant became a full professor at Saint Michael's. He retired in 2002.

Farino Studio

◆ (above left) John Carvellas, professor of economics, began teaching at Saint Michael's in 1974. In addition to teaching, he has also been the chair of the economics department, assistant academic dean and coached women's lacrosse and men's football. He also is recognized as an unofficial "foster parent" of international students. ◆ (above right) Robert Henault taught European history and served as chair of the history department from 1969 to 1972. ◆ (below left) Jim Dillon '32 joined the business and economics faculty after retiring from an executive position at Borden Inc. in 1969. ◆ (below right) Professor of Fine Arts Roy Kennedy, a sculptor, created the three-foot mace used in the College's ceremonial processions. ◆ (facing page) Gregg Blasdel, a renowned sculptor, began teaching at Saint Michael's in 1982. He instructs students in the Sloane Art Center on the historic North Campus at Fort Ethan Allen.

John McKeith

Paul Talley

John McKeith

◆ (above left) Kristin Novotny, professor of political science, began teaching at Saint Michael's in 1993. Her areas of expertise include ancient and modern political theory, socialization and psychology and feminist political theory. ◆ (above right) Academic advising is just one way students interact closely with their professors to help plan their course load each semester. Here, Donna Bozzone, professor of biology, counsels a student. ◆ (below) Reverend Richard L. VanderWeel,

SSE '58, entered the Edmundites in 1955 and took his first vows in August 1956. He began teaching in the College's philosophy department in 1963 and remained a full-time professor until 2002. His charismatic teaching style caused him to be a favorite among students. However, his demanding expectations helped earn him the nickname "VanderFail" over the years.

Bill Denison

John McKeith

◆ (above) Reverend Brian J. Cummings, SSE '86, was ordained by Most Reverend Moses Anderson, SSE '54, on June 15, 1996, and is the youngest member of the Society of Saint Edmund. Besides instructing in business administration and accounting, Reverend Cummings has led the liturgical choir on its annual trip to New Jersey, served as chaplain for the basketball team and the Student Association, and in 2003, was appointed Director of Edmundite Campus Ministry. ◆ (below) F. Nicholas Clary, professor of English, began teaching at the College in 1970 and is a highly regarded and published authority on Shakespeare's *Hamlet*.

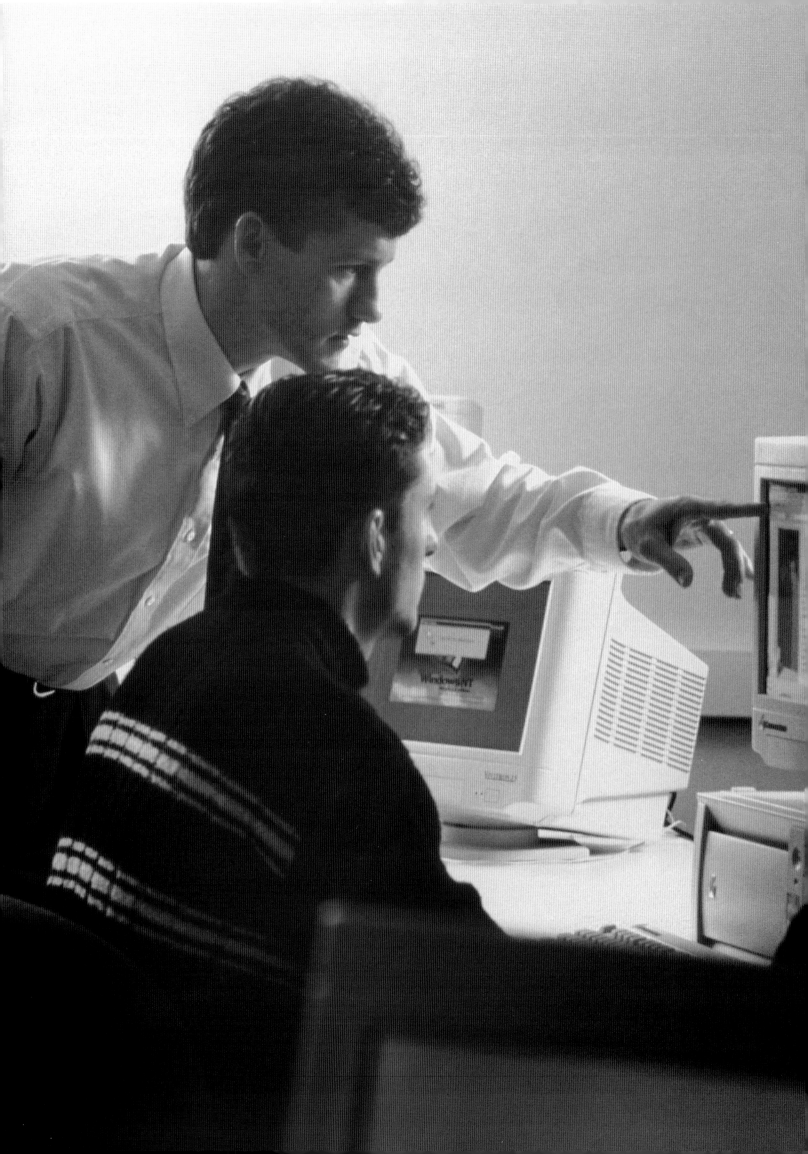

TRADITIONS

William E. Wilson, *Professor of Political Science*

When invited to write on traditions and community at Saint Michael's, I accepted the task with reservation, for to examine community is to run the risk of banality. A computer search, taking less than half a second, yielded greater than 84 million connections based on the word "community." Yet appearances can be deceiving; mere use of the term is no guarantee it exists or prospers within society. Indeed, the frequency of its use may only confirm our collective awareness of its absence. Contemporary critics of American society have recognized the elements of modern life which threaten a sense of community to the detriment of our sense of identity and well-being. To the extent Saint Michael's has prospered as a purposeful community, it has served not only its own members but offered to others a model of what might be and is always becoming. This essay is offered as a complement to a visual "reading" of the College photographs taken over time. With word, and image, and your own experiences, you can engage and touch upon what is special for so many and yet eludes simple definition: the Saint Michael's community.

While "community" holds meaning in all dimensions of learning, it can most easily be associated with the growing understanding of ecology: the interaction of all living things and their environment. Naturalist Aldo Leopold recognized the application of this concept to human

> There is in all visible things
> An invisible fecundity,
> A dimmed light,
> a meek namelessness,
> a hidden wholeness.
> This mysterious, Unity and Integrity
> Is Wisdom, the Mother of all,
> *Natura naturans.*
> *–Thomas Merton*

◆ (facing page) The College is committed to providing students with the best technology and is constantly at work to upgrade and improve its technological infrastructure. Here, Director of Web Site Development Brian MacDonald assists a student in one of the campus' many computer labs. ◆ (right) A Freshman Beanie

of people living together in a place and wishing to continue to do so. To put it another way, a community is a locally understood interdependence of local people, local culture, local economy, and local nature."

This emphasis upon the local engages questions of size and scale. We can think of a functioning human community only in terms of whole relationships among those with shared experiences in a common setting. To this end, and against an array of forces pulling outward, says Berry, "a human

THE MICHAELMAN'S CREED

In union with all the faithful alumni, past and present, I profess my firm belief in the ideals handed down to us by the venerable founders of St. Michael's College. With them I firmly declare that belief in God is the most important and the most influential factor of life. With them I believe that the ideal education has been perfectly realized in the life of Jesus Christ, the second Person of the most Holy Trinity. From Him we have received truths of supreme importance for the whole of life, truths which have given a new meaning to human existence. His coming and His abiding with men through His Church have immeasurably transformed civilization. I acknowledge my debt of gratitude to the founders of our college who have established the means whereby I may attain the ideal of a truly Christian education. Under the patronage of the great Archangel Michael I recognize it as my special duty to be a valiant defender of religion and Christian morality.

I pledge upon my honor to be faithful to the ideals of every loyal son of St. Michael's College. Through work and study and prayer, through the frequentation of the Sacraments, I shall strive always to increase my spirit of faith, and to enrich my character for the greater glory of God and the honor of St. Michael's College. I pledge myself to that code of conduct consistent with these ideals. In return I ask of St. Michael's College, — its faculty, its alumni and all my fellow students to accord me the privilege of the name — MICHAELMAN.

affairs and advocated human ethical understanding be expanded to a "land ethic," which "simply enlarges the boundaries of the community to include soils, waters, plants, and animals, or collectively, the land." While this essay focuses on a college community, its consideration cannot be separated from the wider social and natural environments. Writer Wendell Berry provides a helpful definition:

"By community, I mean the commonwealth and common interests, commonly understood,

Robert Hagerman

community must exert a sort of centripetal force, holding local soil and local memory in place."

Human communities are always rooted in the particular, within boundaries of people and space. It is within this partiality that communities function as a complement to individuals but can also act as metaphors for the universal. The autonomy of individuals falls short of the sense of wholeness to which humans aspire; we are ultimately social animals and draw part of our identity and needed support from that larger but limited group. At the same time, the community can provide a "working notion" of the universal, giving life to the injunction to "think globally, act locally." Thus humans live with paradox in the pursuit of both the individual and community "self."

American higher education has been drawn to the idea of "community." While taking on the general attributes of a community, colleges have focused upon becoming purposeful communities dedicated to

learning. A 1990 Carnegie Foundation report on campus life identified such communities as purposeful and also striving to be "open, just, disciplined, caring, and celebrative." These are widely held goals for institutions of higher education, and they have come to be recognized in a context of learning, which centers on the academic but recognizes the wider learning opportunities of undergraduate life. These expanded dimensions can complement academic life directly as well as contributing to the wider notion of a college community.

Saint Michael's College has long nurtured these ideas as central to its mission. Drawing upon its own nature and experience, the College has been committed to community as a "manifestation of the Edmundite tradition...based on the perspective of the Catholic faith that every human person is fundamentally social, inescapably a member of a community, and that redemption and salvation in Christ is a communal enterprise" (Catalogue, 2001-2003).

Rob Swanson

Such a commitment touches both curriculum and pedagogy deeply. No course of study can move forward without some sense of its implications for society. Over the course of four years, and especially through liberal studies, students come to examine their world as one in which human communities must be honored and nurtured.

There are implications here for both teaching and learning. Educator Parker Palmer has articulated a process of education with community at its core, arguing that "to teach is to create a space in which the community of truth is practiced." Central to this approach to teaching is the notion of dialogue between teacher and student so that at times each assumes the qualities of the other, with truth existing

◆ (facing page) Carl Krauth and his parents of Dedham, Massachusetts are greeted by Dean of Men, Reverend Gerald Duford, as they arrive for Carl's freshman year at Saint Michael's in 1956. ◆ (above and below) Move-In Day

within the dialogue rather than resting in a single source. Such a pedagogy begins in the classroom and permeates all campus life.

This College community has also been shaped by its physical setting. In his study of democracy on a human scale, political scientist Frank Bryan '63 wrote, "Vermont is communal from the ground up. The great glacier that visited 12,000 years ago rolled massive boulders between ice and soil and gouged out hundreds of nesting places for community. Up and down, hill and dale, that is Vermont: a continuing

patchwork of little rivers, small mountains, hollows, ridges, slopes, and bends – perfect places for small settlements. Community life in Vermont is naturally integrated into the one landscape."

To live in Vermont is to be drawn to a human scale, which invites community, and the institutions here are shaped over time by the land and its impact upon people. The land of Saint Michael's was once a farm on fertile land beside a river opening into the valley of Lake Champlain; it was within this setting the founding fathers began the College. Today, the natural environment continues to draw many to Vermont as a working landscape in which the promise of a sustainable environment can be imagined. Community is born of time as well as place. Healthy communities nurture a sense of where they have been and also the possibilities of their future. Saint Michael's has cultivated an awareness of the European roots of

....

◆ (below) At the P-Day Tricycle Race, the faculty-staff softball team The Archangels celebrated their victory, including Bill Anderson, Brian Ortale, Larry Barnes, Rev. Michael Cronogue, SSE and Todd Wadsworth. ◆ (facing page) P-Day is a tradition cherished by students from the College's past and present. Initially, P-Day stood for Preview Day and provided students with a preview of what the larger spring event, Junior Weekend, would offer. Often, the two events had the same theme.

this learning community in times past combined with a recognition of the changes undertaken and those remaining unfinished.

Among the unique qualities of campus communities is both the brevity and intensity of the undergraduate experience. Despite its relatively short duration of four years, the totality of a residential experience focused upon learning helps to create the ties, which often last a lifetime. As many of the images suggest, the traditions of campus life, while modified over time, still respond to the rhythm of four years of active engagement in a purposeful community.

This four-year cycle poses both challenges and opportunities for the vitality of community life. The undergraduate cycle must quickly and fully integrate students into the College. At the same time, each new generation of students provides an infusion of new ideas and attitudes, which keep the community vital and connected to other communities outside the College. In that sense Saint Michael's extends itself over time as its graduates leave and form an extended community, which sustains ties to one another and the College.

It is to state the obvious that we are all members of larger networks and live within multiple communities. Yet true communities deal with whole people, not bundles of functions, that is perhaps their crucial gift to contemporary society. While specialization exercises a centrifugal force upon our roles as family members, professionals, and students, the community strives to create an opposing force which draws to the center and holds in balance our separateness. As graduates leave the College and enter the larger world, they carry with them a sense of the possibility of community. More than any single component or partiality of their life at Saint Michael's, what remains is the comfort of the broader and deeper relationships with others.

The relationships between students, faculty, and staff are at the core of these memories. Years after graduation, students remember advisor meetings or a particular class discussion. They recall offhand

comments by professors, forgotten by the source but vivid to the listener. They remember sharing the dreams of youth with friends and are sustained by classmates as those dreams become reality. Service trips and off-campus studies all take place within a supporting framework which encourages risk but seeks to cushion failure. The comradeship of athletic contests, dramatic productions and concerts shape the recollection of important moments. All of these disparate threads of memory are woven into a tapestry of community life.

It would be wrong to discount the importance of the "natural community" to the sense of wholeness. The quiet beauty of the Winooski River and its fields, and the drama of mountains to the east and west are

a comfort for many. The rhythm of the seasons shapes the rhythm of the academic year as well. Few who have left the College do not carry with them the feel of brisk mornings of fall and the warmth of afternoon sun. The severity and duration of winters grow to legend, and there is always the celebration of the first warm days of spring, regardless of the month. For all this, many define our community as Saint Michael's College "in Vermont."

Observers often comment on the connectedness of our work, joining together faculty and students and staff in the educational enterprise both inside the classroom and beyond. Such work can prosper only in a community of learners where each skill and virtue is valued but never separated from the wholeness of the person. It is that quality of acceptance which allows all to know themselves and also recognize this community as a part of their larger being, and so draw together small things into the whole. ◆

....

◆ (facing page) Climbing a greased pole was a longstanding P-Day tradition. ◆ (below) Students engage in a mock battle on P-Day 1962.

◆ (above) King and Queen of the Winter Carnival John Terezini and Peg Gilbert ◆ (below) Choosing a prom queen ◆ (facing page) In 1980, after thirty years, *The Michaelman* student newspaper was renamed *The Defender*. Today, *The Defender* remains a tradition, published weekly by a student staff. *The Echo*, an online media student publication, began in 2001.

The Defender

Bishop speaks about homosexuality in the church, Page 11 | Baseball team itching to hit the field, Page 16

Volume XXX, Issue 6

March 26, 2003 — St. Michael's College Student Newspaper

President unve[ils]
SMC's 'master [plan]'

Possible projects: Parking garage, rink, new dorms

By Josh Kessler
News Editor

Major construction could occur at St. Michael's within the next 25 years. Such projects as building a new road to North Campus, rerouting the campus road and building a second athletic complex are in the works.

President Marc vander-Heyden presented possible campus changes to the Student Association on March 18 as a preliminary step in the school's master plan. VanderHeyden will officially propose the master plan to the board of trustees when it visits on April 4-5.

VanderHeyden was careful to point out he was "only taking inventory" of campus alterations suggested during the past 10 years.

While most changes have been neither approved nor offi-

cially presented to the board of trustees, vanderHeyden suggested the campus's landscape could change dramatically while enrollment would remain at about 1,800 students.

The major projects include building a road from Main Campus to North Campus goes through St. Michael's-owned Winchester Place. The plan avoids Vermont 15. The project would require Camp John...move its entrance 200...back from the road, some...has agreed to do. St. M...owns the land occupied...camp's entrance.

Other projects have...cussed, including:

• Rerouting the...road behind the...Education Center so...with the 300s Tow...and continues beh...Recreation Center.

• Building a...at the location of the...n's courts.

• Burying the...Vermont 15 and...way.

ROT[C]

Bush visits Vermont

College hosts dinner

by Randy Walker

About 10 peaceful campus protesters, including at least three St. Michael's College resident assistants, joined another 100 students in greeting Republican vice-presidential candidate George Bush in front of the Ross Sport Center on Friday, Sept. 26.

Shaking outstretched hands and commenting on the cold Vermont weather, Bush spent less than five minutes with the mildly enthusiastic crowd as a tight circle of Secret Service agents and aggressive network camera crewmen edged him toward the entrance of the building.

Inside, the politician addressed an estimated 927 guests at a $50-a-plate Vermont Republican dinner. The event netted his party nearly $35,000, according to one Bush staffer.

Bush attacked Carter's economic and foreign rela-

tions policies as being weak, noting that "neither Kennedy, Mondale, nor Carter were able to defend the president's record/ during the National Democratic Convention."

Bush dismissed Carter's recent allegation that the fall election will offer voters "a choice between war and peace," citing Reagan's superior knowledge of the "intent of Soviet leadership" as a positive factor in the maintenance of peace.

"On the economic front, specifics of Mr. Reagan's tax cut proposals have been a matter of public record for over two weeks now," Bush said, adding that now Carter camp criticism of 'the plan that will not work' has ceased," Bush said.

He told his receptive silver-haired audience that winning a Republican senate majority in November was of "paramount" importance to successful implementa-

tion of Reagan economic policies.

But Bush's reception by students outside the building had not been as warm. Silent protesters held placards with such slogans as "The only Bush we'll swallow is beer" and "Bush — Head for the Mountains."

College President Edward L. Henry, on hand to greet the Republican leader, expressed support for the protesters. "I'd be disappointed if the students didn't have enough guts to express themselves here tonight," Henry said.

After receiving an SMC windbreaker, Bush was introduced to G.A. executive board members Molly Dwyer, Maureen Sullivan, and Michele Kramer.

The politician quipped that the board was discriminatory, a political gaffe in light of staunch Reagan opposition to the proposed Equal Rights Amendment.

cont. on page 20

To rally support of GOP party members, former ambassador George Bush, Republican vice-presidential candidate, attacked Carter's economic policies at the Ross Sport Center Friday night. *photo by David Walsh*

Vol. 1 No. 4   October 3, 1980   Saint Michael's College   Winooski, Vermont 05404

The Defender

Proposed doctoral program draws faculty criticism

by Brenda Berry

A new doctoral program...

...ty meeting last week. The program would consist of one third...

...that the faculty "appeared to be...

...oral...ohn...of ...ity ...the ...ed" ...ere ...was ...ag-

...ng-...iss ...on, ...rs-...ly ...ra-...ll

that emphasis should be placed instead on better undergraduate programs in all departments.

"The present certification program and the M.A. programs in the Department of Education fail to do an adequate job of teaching because they are understaffed," Reiss said. Education instructors are now overextended . . ."

According to Reiss, the main objective of the proposed program is to make money. Stockton denied that claim, saying the main purpose of the program is to "enhance the image of SMC

by being a quality program and a source of support for the undergraduate education program."

Reiss said the education staff is over extended, and the graduate program is "mediocre" at best. "We have no business in starting a doctoral program," he protested. "To anyone who knows anything about education, the program would be a farce."

According to Stockton, the education program is at a developmental stage right now, "functioning at a level slightly above rumor." He

---

"Good losers get into the habit of losing."
George E. Allen

Michaelman

Saint Michael's College, Winooski, Vermont.

Vol. 35 No. 3   September 21, 1979

Special events highlight jubilee year

by Tom Liptak

The 1979-80 school year has begun, and with it, the continuation of the 75th Jubilee Anniversary celebration, featuring a host of academic symposiums, lectures, plays, concerts and arts-related events.

The jubilee "year" actually began in January 1979 and will carry through to November 1980, a span of almost two years. The reason for that, according to Dr. Richard McDowell, the jubilee's director, is that the school was founded during a period that spanned more than one year.

A simple glance at the jubilee celebration's schedule of events, however, makes it plain that it would be quite difficult, if not impossible, to fit all the activities already staged, and those that are forthcoming, into a span of only one year.

The first major jubilee event this year will be a symposium entitled "The Citizen Soldier in Today's World," to be held Oct. 5 and 6. This conference will be composed of 11 panels and related bookings which

will address issues such as the all-volunteer army, the reinstitution of the draft, women in the military, and modern warfare, to name only a few.

St. Michael's was founded in 1903-1904 by priests of the Society of St. Edmund. They had relocated in northern Vermont after leaving France in the early 1900s. The Edmundites were educators in France.

With about $1,300 in donations and some of their own funds they bought the land on which Founders Hall is built. The site included a two-story farm house and three barns.

The college began as "St. Michael's Institute," but became St. Michael's College in 1913. Only 33 students were enrolled for the first year the school was open, 1904-1905. At the time, St. Michael's was both a college and a prep school, although the prep school was dropped in 1931. By 1940 there were 250 students enrolled.

After the war, the number of students increased rapidly as veterans decided to attend college under their G.I. bene-

fits. Several buildings from Fort Ethan Allen (now the north campus) were brought to the main campus to be used as offices, classrooms and dorms. Many of these buildings have since been torn down.

In these years, St. Michael's also began a major building project. The four quad dorms were constructed in the 1950s and '60s. Alliot, Durick Library, Ross Sports Center and McCarthy Arts Center were all built in the 1960s and early '70s, gradually replacing the all-purpose Jemery Hall.

The nature of St. Michael's was changed even more in 1970 when the first 23 women were admitted to the college. Now the student body is almost half female.

Another jubilee event that is already in progress is The Einstein Centennial Exhibit sponsored by Dr. Edward Foley and the physics department. The exhibit will run through Sept. 21 in the McCarthy Arts Center.

Events scheduled through Homecoming Weekend, Oct. 19-21, include:

A discussion on American higher education entitled,

"The Liberal Arts, in Crisis", sponsored by the humanities department; Sept. 20. A symposium entitled "Collective Bargaining and Dispute Settlement in the 1980s, sponsored by the business department, in which panels and related bookings will address themselves to increasing the participants' knowledge of the skills required in the collective

bargaining process in both the public and private . sectors; Oct. 12-13. A symposium entitled "Society and Secularization," sponsored by the sociology and religious studies departments; Oct. 17-18. The Hartnett lectures in which alumni in the fields of medicine and biological research will discuss related topics.

Tickets for 1980 Winter Olympics to go on sale soon at St. Mike's

You probably figured that, as usual, you'd be watching the winter olympic games, coming up early next year, on your lounge television or in some bar. Well, if you can beat the lines into Director of Student Activities Jennifer Cernosia's office, you may just be able to see some of the world's best athletes in person at Lake Placid, NY.

Thanks to the Student Life Office and the social committee, tickets for the 1980 Winter Olympics will go on sale to St. Michael's students and faculty

on a first-come, first-served basis in the near future.

According to Cernosia, a package of two events including transportation from Burlington to Lake Placid will cost from $58.45 to $81.85. All the tickets will go on sale at one time, and Cernosia said she expected to sell all the tickets in a short time.

She said that a ticket limit would probably be set so that a few people would not be able to buy all the tickets. A St. Michael's College I.D. must be shown to purchase a package.

...entertained St. Michael's swillers at the Craftsbury Fair this weekend. *photo by Buffy Pennick*

1979-80 academic and jubilee year celebration calendar

1979 FALL SEMESTER

September 29	Feast of St. Michael Festival Mass, classes as usual	14-15	The Future of American Foreign Policy: a symposium	grades from previous semester
October 5-6	The Citizen Soldier in Today's World...	16	Feast of St. Edmund, special Mass, classes as usual	29 Spring recess begins after last class March Can Local Government Survive? a symposium (date to be an...

◆ (above) Baseball jersey worn by varsity players during the 1950s. ◆ (below left and right) Saint Michael's Letter Jacket and shortsleeved jacket ◆ (facing page above) On February 26, 1960, the College Glee Club presented a joint concert with the legendary Louis Armstrong at Burlington's Memorial Auditorium. The Glee Club then cut a record with RCA Victor. ◆ (facing page below right) In 1947, students published the first annual yearbook, the *Shield*. In 1973, its name was changed to *The Hilltop*. ◆ (facing page below left) A Junior Weekend souvenir. The Junior Weekend theme, "Al Jaharah," was suggested by international students who offered the Arabian theme to the committee. The Saudi Arabian embassy in Washington, DC, became upset about the College using the names of their sacred events for a party weekend, prompting former College attorney Tom Kenney '50 and an international student to go to Washington to make amends.

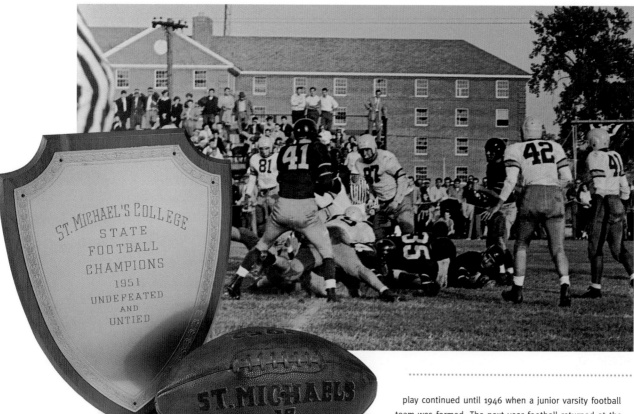

◆ (above) The outdoor ice rink, pictured in 1951, provided opportunities to face-off against other colleges or to just play pick-up games throughout the winter. Often plagued by poor ice conditions, many hockey games were cancelled each year. ◆ (center) In 1933, football was dropped as a varsity sport because of expense. Inter-class play continued until 1946 when a junior varsity football team was formed. The next year football returned at the varsity level. In January 1954 President Moriarty announced that, again, "Football is a luxury a small liberal arts college can't afford." The sport was viewed by the trustees as a financial drain and was said to be one of the contributing factors hindering the College from expanding its physical facilities. In the late 1960s students again petitioned for football to come back on a club basis, and it was played on varsity level with other club teams until 1978. ◆ (below) The College's 1951 football team, led by Doc Jacobs, went undefeated and untied, ultimately winning the New England Championship.

◆ (above) Fans flocked to Evansville, Indiana, to watch the Knights compete in the national basketball finals. In 1959, students embarked on a road trip of nearly 1,300 miles to support their team. ◆ (below left) 1953 basketball standouts Chris Kelly and Hank White ◆ (below right) The 1957-1958 basketball team finished second nationally and were the NCAA Northeast Champs. This basketball, from that season, is signed by the entire team.

◆ (facing page above) Saint Michael's fans rooting for their team at a 1950 basketball game versus the University of Vermont. The Knights stopped the Cats' advances with a 56-52 win that brought the Knights the state title. ◆ (facing page below left) Away jersey worn by Rich Tarrant '65. Rich scored 1,762 career points while at Saint Michael's and was a fourth-round pick by the Boston Celtics in the 1965 NBA draft. Tarrant was a College Hall of Fame inductee in 1987, and his number, 22, has been retired from active use. ◆ (facing page below center) Size 16 basketball shoes worn by 6'10" center Ken Johnson '76. ◆ (facing page below right) Various basketball trophies ◆ (above) In January 1965, over 3,000 attended a "Doc" tribute held at Burlington's Memorial Auditorium. Doc Jacobs retired in 1964 after 18 years as head coach to devote himself full-time to his job as athletic director of intercollegiate and intramural athletics. Here he is receiving congratulations from Vermont's Governor Philip Hoff. ◆ (right) George W. "Doc" Jacobs (right) with Barry Branon '36. He earned his nickname, Doc, because of his love of books, according to a 1961 issue of *The Michaelman*. Jacobs, who began at Saint Michael's in 1947, was noted as one of New England's top basketball coaches.

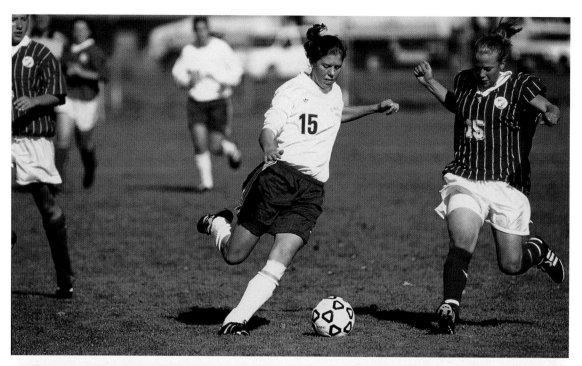

◆ (facing page above) Women's soccer ◆ (facing page below) Cheerleaders from the 1970s ◆ (above left) Edward Patrick Markey Jr. '51 (left), served as athletic director for 29 years before retiring in 1997. Markey is pictured with Sue Duprat, who arrived at Saint Michael's in 1976. Duprat served for 27 years as head of the College's women's basketball program before retiring in 2003. ◆ (above right) Each year, Saint Michael's elects outstanding athletes into the Athletic Hall of Fame and honors each recipient with a medal and an induction ceremony. This medal was given in abstentia to Julian Miller '11. Miller was the College's first African-American student and was a standout as halfback on the football team. He also demonstrated academic prowess in the classroom and, while a freshman, won a gold medal for elocution. Miller was a founding member of the Newman Lyceum Honor Society at Saint Michael's. ◆ (below) A packed night at Ross Sports Center in 1989, with almost a sell-out crowd cheering on their Purple Knights.

Paul Talley

Paul Boisvert

◆ (facing page above) The 1988 women's field hockey team was led to their NCAA Division II championship title with Parry Porter '89 as all-time leading scorer. ◆ (facing page below) Field Hockey Championship program and trophies ◆ (above) Women's field hockey ◆ (below) Team photo from the first women's ice hockey club team at the College in 1996-97. Lady Ice Knights, front row (from left to right): Kelly Taylor '00, Annmarie Rizzotti '98, Sarah Roda '97, Kristy Sweeney '98, Liz Zona '98, Holly Cressman '98; second row,

Brian Ruck '98 and Steve Mattson, assistant coaches; Bridget Risley '97, Sarah Foley '99, Jill Trongo '99, Sarah Blodgett '98, Amy Peters '99, Melanie Beach '99, Carol McCrorey '97, Sue Creedon '99, Reverend Marcel Rainville, SSE '67, team chaplain; Judy Valente '96, coach; third row, Heather Lewis '99, Gretchen Hooper '98, Danielle Grondin '98, Heather Murray '99, Tara Feeney '99, Wendy Shepard '99, and Shelley Smith '97.

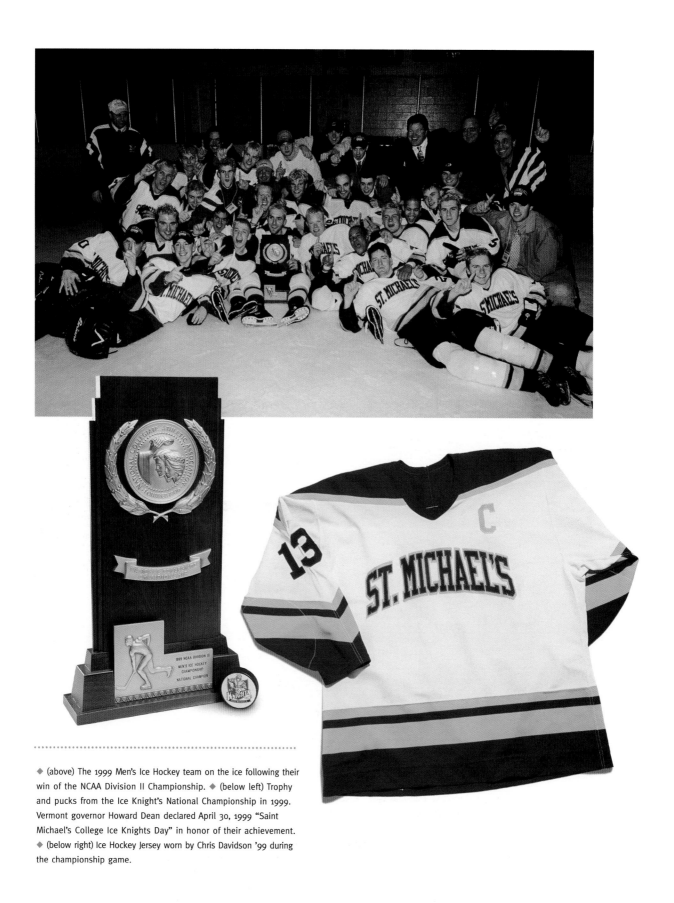

◆ (above) The 1999 Men's Ice Hockey team on the ice following their win of the NCAA Division II Championship. ◆ (below left) Trophy and pucks from the Ice Knight's National Championship in 1999. Vermont governor Howard Dean declared April 30, 1999 "Saint Michael's College Ice Knights Day" in honor of their achievement. ◆ (below right) Ice Hockey Jersey worn by Chris Davidson '99 during the championship game.

Dana Lim vanderHeyden

EN MÉMOIRE
DES PÈRES DE SAINT-EDME
DE PONTIGNY
FONDATEURS EN 1867
DE L'ARCHICONFRÉRIE
DE SAINT MICHEL

Dana Lim vanderHeyden

◆ (above) During the first pilgrimage to France in 1998, Edmundite priests from Saint Michael's concelebrated Mass at the high altar of the abbey church of Mont-Saint-Michel, the very abbey the Edmundites helped to restore in the late nineteenth century. Trips abroad to examine the College's earliest roots have since become a yearly tradition for groups of Edmundites, alumni, trustees, faculty and staff. Since 2002, they have included traveling to England to study Saint Edmund's earliest beginnings as well. ◆ (below) In July 1997, Marc and Dana vanderHeyden traveled to Pontigny to explore the roots of Saint Michael's founding order, a trip that led to the creation of Pontigny Pilgrimages. One year later, in July 1998, the first official pilgrimage group from the College traveled to France. While there, they discovered a unique connection at Mont-Saint-Michel in Madame Helene Lebrec, whose grandparents played a very important role for the Edmundite community in the early 1900s. Pictured here is Madame Lebrec, with Reverends Richard Berube, SSE and Marcel Rainville, SSE.

Harry Richards

◆ (facing page) Knight's armor on display in the Tarrant Center ◆ (above) Bagpipers lead the presidential inauguration procession to Ross Sports Center for the installation of Marc A. vanderHeyden as the College's fifteenth president on October 19, 1996. ◆ (below)

Members of the class of 1948 process by the construction of Cheray Science Hall. The building was dedicated on May 15, 1949 to the memory of Reverend Louis M. Cheray, SSE. Cheray was a professor of science, Latin and mathematics from 1904 to 1908.

◆ (facing page above) The parents of Marcel Le Blanc '50 greet their son following commencement. ◆ (facing page below) Commencement 1957 ◆ (above) Commencement was held on the steps of the Durick Library throughout the 1970s. ◆ (below) The Mill in Winooski was home to many good times for Saint Michael's students across the decades. In 1967, David Trieber, John Clark, Jim McKearin, SSE, Bart Federici and Phil celebrate commencement at the haunt.

OUR SECOND CENTURY

Marc A. vanderHeyden, *President*

At the beginning of its second century, Saint Michael's College can look back at an incredible legacy and tradition in order to be informed and encouraged to look forward with faith, hope and determination. All colleges, indeed all organizations, have to prepare for their future, but it is equally true that to dream, think and plan, it is critically important to be knowledgeable, appreciative and even enamored of the past.

Therefore, at Saint Michael's College, we must remember Saint Edmund, we must remember the Cistercian tradition of Pontigny, we must remember the appeal of Mont-Saint-Michel, and we must remember the Society of Saint Edmund, our founders and models in life. From each and every part of our heritage, we need to learn and embrace key precepts that will ensure the continued success of Saint Michael's College.

From Saint Edmund, we take a devotion to learning —open-minded and open-ended—and a parallel devotion to teaching that embodies a deep love for both students and scholarship. We also know from him that study of the liberal arts is central, indeed pivotal, to all learning that prepares students for fulfilling lives.

In addition, Saint Edmund helps us realize that to study in community is the best way to assure the growth of mind and character. Hence, Saint Michael's College strives to ensure that the quality of the residential life experience is comparable to the excellence

John McKeith

◆ (facing page) The 420 undergraduate students of the Class of 2003 process to the Ross Sports Center on May 11, 2003 for Saint Michael's ninety-sixth commencement exercises. Loung Ung '93, a national spokeswoman for the Vietnam Veterans of America Foundation's Campaign for a Land Mine Free World, addressed the graduates. ◆ (above) Saint Michael's embraces its Catholic heritage today as proudly as it has for its entire 100-year history. Reverend Marcel Rainville, SSE '67, director of Edmundite Campus Ministry until 2003, talks with students teaching in the family religious education program, one of the many benefits that Campus Ministry offers to the local worshipping community.

we pursue in our intellectual endeavors—learning together is matched by learning to live together.

Finally, Saint Edmund models for us the virtues of serving one another. He attended to students at Oxford, poor people as a parish priest, and the issues of the king, the realm and the Church as Archbishop of Canterbury. To learn to serve the poor and the mighty has to be part of a complete education at Saint Michael's College. We will then find that a life dedicated to knowledge, service and our Creator can be fulfilling, even saintly, and demonstrates the continued growth of a human being.

From the Cistercians, we do well to accept the importance of silence and prayer, contemplation and reflection, giving of the self and a self-effacing demeanor that leads to a soul filled with spirit. The need for introspection may become even more acute

in the decades to come. Our students, faculty and staff will need moments of rest in an environment that will be plagued by an overload of technology and distractions, that is surrounded by vulgarity disguised as freedom, and that removes us from the very core of being human. This is the strain in the fabric of our legacy which calls us to become spiritual, and while it may cause some to argue the limited relevance of spirituality in an environment that grows ever more secular, it will be important for an institution of higher learning to continue this debate.

From Mont-Saint-Michel—whence comes the College's name—we must always remember that it was and is an attraction to pilgrims. Therefore, it

◆ The natural beauty of Saint Michael's carefully landscaped campus is evident during each season.

symbolizes the way we will walk through life. Each of us is on a pilgrimage with many stops that will allow us to grow, become better human beings, gain more knowledge and provide greater service to others.

The concept of pilgrimage is very appropriate at the beginning of the twenty-first century. As an individual, and also as a member of a community of learners, we are indeed on the road to growth, knowledge and understanding. It is a compelling image not only for life, but for the pursuit of knowledge and truth, and in the latter, we will find that the path we walk will always be a design crafted from what we learn by reason and what we know by faith—that, too, will give us the tension that makes for great intellectual and life experience.

All of these traditions are integral parts of the intellectual legacy that Saint Michael's College has inherited through the generosity of its founders, the Edmundites. From their history and living examples of service, we gain respect for every person, dedication to a life that is all-encompassing and without compromise, appreciation of knowledge, devotion to the call of religion, and commitment to help the poor and downtrodden and to love one another. From the Edmundites, we learn that humility does not preclude greatness, hospitality is to be offered without limit, and recognition of "otherness" in our fellow human beings is critical to our own self-knowledge and acceptance of the transcendent in our lives.

These are the values that need to permeate Saint Michael's College in its second century. This will not be easy because, simultaneously and with equal depth of conviction, the College must pursue academic excellence, the definition of which will change according to the needs of the times and our society, but will always have the study of humanities at its very core. Study of the humanities will also be the best platform for Saint Michael's to continue its search for identity as a Catholic institution.

The humanities will not only be the basis, but also the target, and will always sustain individual growth and respect for life. The humanist tradition will force this small, independent, Catholic, residential college to seek and implement a human dimension to everything we contemplate, plan, and undertake. Many in the academic community, who worry about the future of "the university"—which has been part of our civilization for 800 years—cannot avoid or circumvent the very fact that all study must begin with the humanities,

no matter what changes may occur in the structure of higher education.

The liberal arts, which have for centuries formed the basis of academic institutions, must always be open to the inclusion of new subject matter, new venues for learning, new ways of teaching and new methods of discovery. A truly liberally educated person will always be curious—committed to informed scrutiny and asking questions. Hence, Saint Michael's second century as a liberal arts institution will always entail subjects and courses of study that keep the College contemporary, but never relinquish the fundamental tradition of critical thinking, free expression, thoughtful inquiry and the pursuit of learning that has proven valuable over the span of human history.

◆ (above) Adrie Kusserow, Saint Michael's College associate professor of anthropology, pictured with her son, Will, was named the 2002 Vermont Professor of the Year by CASE (Council for the Advancement and Support of Education) and the Carnegie Foundation for the Advancement of Teaching. ◆ (facing page) The Saint Michael's College Edmundite Community 2003. Back Row: Reverend Michael P. Cronogue, Very Reverend Richard M. Myhalyk, Reverend Paul E. Couture, Reverend Joseph M. McLaughlin, and Reverend Brian J. Cummings. Front Row: Reverend Richard N. Berube, Reverend Richard L. VanderWeel, Reverend Romeo A. Trahan, Reverend Marcel R. Rainville, and Reverend Raymond J. Doherty.

It is important for a liberal arts institution to accept and admit to the necessity to grow in different directions than may currently be evident. Certain academic disciplines will surface that have yet to be invented and still others may disappear, so a careful mix of these disciplines will constitute the proper liberal arts environment. The need to incorporate the sciences, technology and contemporary subject matter that is relevant to a global society will always put stress on curriculum, faculty and students. We should invite this kind of challenge. Therefore, we will always try to be an institution that, while it is steeped in and devoted to strong traditions, is also open to the introduction of subjects that are new, good, human and important for the next generation to learn.

In this increasingly pluralistic, global society in which we live, Saint Michael's College will need to continue to maintain and manifest the key beliefs of our Catholic tradition, the instructions of the Church, the value of the liberal arts, and the acceptance and scrutiny of new knowledge. This commitment must be shared by all who wish to become a part of this learning community.

It is equally important that those who do not share our values are welcome in our midst, so that we learn from them and they from us, so we enrich one another and so we practice the true ecumenical spirit that characterizes both the Church and any intellectual environment that is truly humanistic and concerned about all. It is only by inclusion that we will learn jointly to find solutions for the problems facing mankind. It is only by learning together that we will also come to appreciate the combination of multiple disciplines in the pursuit of truth and solution. It is only by learning from others and being respectful of their opinions that we can justify articulating our own views. It is critical that the growth of the intellect and adherence to the traditional values we hold dear are always combined in an honest harmony that can tolerate tension and success because such learners will always understand that this kind of study makes life worthwhile, meaningful and divine. ◆

◆ (above) As part of an ambitious residence hall construction project, Cashman Hall was dedicated on October 19, 2002 in memory of the late Edmund J. Cashman, Jr. '58. Throughout his life, Ed Cashman provided tremendous leadership and generosity to Saint Michael's. Cashman Hall houses approximately 124 students living in suites. ◆ (below) As Saint Michael's fifteenth president, Marc A. vanderHeyden has worked to ensure that the College retains its small, Catholic, residential character as it enters the next century. President vanderHeyden and his wife Dana meet with student Centennial Ambassadors and staff from the Centennial committee to discuss plans for the College's upcoming 100-year celebration. ◆ (next spread) "It is our hope and vision that our gift will allow the College to thrive in today's competitive environment, attracting students who, after a Saint Michael's education, will add value to our world," said Bob Hoehl '63 who, with his wife, Cynthia M'90, made a gift of $2.1 million to fund the construction of a new admission facility. The Hoehl Welcome Center serves not only as a new "front door" to the College but as a door ushering Saint Michael's College into its second century.

ACKNOWLEDGEMENTS

This book was produced in collaboration with many offices, departments, staff and faculty members at Saint Michael's College. In particular, we are grateful to Shaun Bryer '03, who spent much of his senior year at Saint Michael's in the archives, with the cooperation and research of Elizabeth Scott, archivist, combing through hundreds of photographs. The photo selection committee of Buff Lindau, Patrick Gallivan '89, Richard DiVenere '67, Jacqueline Murphy '74, Reverend Ray Doherty '51 and Professor Emeritus Daniel Bean did their best to ensure that as many of Saint Michael's important people and places as possible were included. Terryl Kinder, the Cistercian architectural historian, supplied us with additional photos of Pontigny and Mont-Saint-Michel. Anne Conaway Peters deftly managed the project's mechanics and Caroline Crawford kept a close eye on the editorial process, writing and rewriting captions until the eleventh hour. President Marc vanderHeyden, Dana Lim vanderHeyden, Marilyn Cormier and the staff of the President's Office and the Centennial Committee were enthusiastic and encouraging throughout the book's production. And Duane Wood and the entire staff of WDG Communications helped make this daunting project not only manageable but enjoyable.

Most of all, we are grateful to the Edmundite community, who had the vision to found Saint Michael's College one hundred years ago and who continue to be the guiding presence on our College's present and future.

INDEX